P9-BJI-547

What They're Saying ...

Jim Laughren's very readable book provides a wealth of information about the worlds of beer and wine, and a very useful bridge between the two. My first love will always be great craft beer, but Jim certainly helped round-out my appreciation for the world's other great beverage. This is a book that will be read in its entirety and then brought back out to answer questions and settle disputes raised over many bottles of great beer and great wine. Cheers to that!

Dan Kenary, President and Co-Founder,
Harpoon Brewery

Wine and beer are the world's two oldest and most important beverages. Finally here's a book that respects, appreciates and gives both their due. *A Beer Drinker's Guide To Knowing & Enjoying Fine Wine* is excellent. If you're a beer drinker you already know about fermentation, flavors and aromas; now let author and wine expert Jim Laughren reveal the secrets of great wine—how it's made, where it's found and how to maximize your enjoyment of it. This book is a "must read" for anyone, beer drinker or not, who wants to increase their knowledge of fine wine. It's probably the best, and certainly the least snobby, introduction to wine on the market today.

Shields Hood, CWE, CSS, Past President,
Society of Wine Educators

Jim Laughren's no-nonsense approach to these two marvelous beverages leaves no room for swill, yet elevates both great beer and exceptional wine to the levels they deserve. His love of beer and obvious expertise in all things vinous allows him to pull back the veil on the world of fine wine, while at the same time celebrating the best of brewing. *A Beer Drinker's Guide To Knowing & Enjoying Fine Wine* is the ideal starting point to learn more about the world's 'other' great beverage.

Jeff Erway, President and Head Brewer,
La Cumbre Brewing Co.

Jim Laughren dives into the world of fermentable beverages and comes up a winner. Unpretentious and utterly enjoyable, *A Beer Drinker's Guide to Knowing & Enjoying Fine Wine* is masterfully written—a true imbiber's fun and friendly exploration into wine, beer, and exciting wine cocktails. Research and recipes go hand in hand so discover what Jim already knows: wine is for enjoying, so enjoy "mixing it up!"

Linda Pettine, CWE, CSS, Professor of Mixology,
Johnson & Wales University

A Beer Drinker's Guide To Knowing & Enjoying Fine Wine scores a bulls-eye for anyone wanting to explore the ins and outs of wine. Though author and certified wine educator Jim Laughren uses beer and ale as a starting point, his conversational, easy-to-understand style makes this a book for anyone seeking entrée to the world of wine. From styles and varietals to scoring, storing and wine-speaking with the best of the insiders, this book is both fun and truly educational.

Jane Nickles, CWE, author of "WineSpeak 101"

A Beer Drinker's Guide To Knowing And Enjoying Fine Wine

Jim Laughren, CWE

CROSSTOWN PUBLISHING

Portland, Oregon

Maps by Christa Wilson
Illustrations by Charles Somerville
Cover design by www.KarrieRoss.com
Front cover photo by Kate Laughren

Library of Congress Catalog Number: 2012908979
ISBN: 978-0-9855336-1-8

Crosstown Publishing, Inc.
www.crosstownpublishinginc.com
Printed in the United States of America

For Patti,
Always by my side

And Kate,
Always in my heart

Table of Contents

Introduction

"Of course I drink wine. How could I not? Anyone who enjoys aromas and flavours must find enjoyment in both of the world's two great fermented drinks."

...the late, great Michael Jackson, international beer expert

So, it's finally time to get serious, to stop fooling around. No one says you have to give up beer—like that's ever going to happen—but.... Was it the lady in your life who suggested it? Or maybe the husband or boyfriend, or someone at work talking about that new wine bar down the street. It might even have been your boss, or those think-they're-all-that friends, who keep trying to get you into wine.

But why? you ask. Because, they say. You're missing out; it's time you showed a little, well, sophistication (as if they had any of their own). It's time your palate grew up. Or, says the boss, we'd like you to entertain some clients but they're looking for a more ... upscale experience. Or because you moved to that hip new neighborhood and when you get invited to parties or get-togethers, everyone's standing around sipping glasses of red or white, not frothy amber. Or maybe you'd like to find a partner and it's dawned on you that wine tastings can be great venues for slightly tipsy encounters of the possibly romantic kind. And you're right—drinking wine can be a delicious way to meet smart, interesting and yes, attractive people. To expand your circle, not to mention the old horizons. To learn something new and worthwhile and easier on the shins and fingernails than rock-wall climbing at the gym. Or maybe you're thinking that wine could be *almost* as interesting as some of the terrific new craft brews you've been enjoying. And let's be honest, what wine you've had, you've liked. Maybe you haven't sampled that much, not of the really good stuff, but most of the juice you've tried has been pretty tasty. So why not uncover its secrets? Explore a little. Take a walk on the vino side of the street. Welcome to the wonderful world of wine.

Is there anything better on a hot summer's day after a sweaty afternoon pushing a lawnmower around the postage stamp or finishing a three-lost-balls round of golf in the midday sun than an icy cold lager? The answer, as every beer drinker knows, is "of course not." Nothing quenches that deep-down, hard-work thirst like a frosty mug of liquid nectar.

Lovely, delicious, and refreshing. From pale ale to a rich, heady stout, nothing fills the bill like a great beer when it comes to satisfying a big thirst. From toasty to nutty, from sweet to sour, with a dose of caramel, a hit of hops, or a dash of fruit, good beer offers a dazzling array of flavors that only adds to its enjoyment.

And yet, as good as the properly chosen brew can be, especially with a hefty meat and cheese or a sizzling burger off the grill, even the most ardent hops fan will be amazed at the incredible range of styles—the diversity of the flavors, textures and aromas—found in the world's other great beverage. For those into the grape, nothing is more versatile, more complex, more damned delicious, glass after glass, than a well-made, well-chosen wine.

Now hold on! Don't get yourself all in a froth, there. And don't even think about hurling that heirloom stein at me. What is, is. And just as beer in all its manifestations, from pilsner to porter, from doppelbocks to double IPAs, makes for a remarkable gallery of taste and satisfaction, wine's range of styles, types, colors, tastes, and aromas makes it a beverage worthy of study and imbibing by even the world's greatest brew lovers. Consider the influence of tens, if not hundreds of thousands of vineyard sites, of thousands of grape varieties, of uncountable variations in soil and weather conditions, of the umpteen winemaking decisions that vary not only from vintner to vintner but from day to day during the growing season, the winemaking process, and even during the aging regimen—and the potential for beautiful outcomes is unlimited. Not to mention the annual shifting of all the rules and possibilities due to vintage variation.

Also a product of fermentation, think of wine like beer's first cousin. Both have histories going back thousands of years. Both are agricultural products, one from grains, the other from grapes. Both have played major roles in rituals and celebrations and plain old good times in countless civilizations covering every corner of the globe for longer than recorded history. And both challenge the senses with complexities of taste and aroma that vodka, fruit juice or soft drink lovers will never know.

Another element common to both beer and wine is the passion of their devotees. Each group reveres their beverage of choice, for various reasons, as the one "true" drink, the "if you had to spend the rest of your life on a desert island" choice. And yet, it takes practice and paying attention to become a true aficionado. Anyone can suck down a six-pack of cheap factory lager or polish off a jug of better-left-untouched "plonk" and wake up with a nasty hangover the next day; no particular talent required. But those who really appreciate what they're drinking have learned to pay attention and so their palates pick up the subtleties and nuances that transform swilling into savoring.

What this means is 1.) that wine drinkers can probably detect the nuances in a good beer faster and more easily than non-beer drinkers, and 2.) that hops fans can learn the ins and outs, the secret codes and complexities of wine at a greatly accelerated pace vis-à-vis the rest of the world.

So whether it's your friends, your business associates or simply your own gustatory curiosity that's nudging you in the direction of wine, of becoming more familiar and conversant with this magnificent libation, take heart all ye lovers of grain, for we're about to make the journey into wine easier and more fun than you ever thought possible!

■ ■ ■ ■

1

A Different Way of Drinking:
An Introduction to Wine-Think

Lager, lambic, ale, pilsner, porter, stout, bock, bitter, red beer, white beer, ice beer, steam beer—most beer drinkers have heard of some or all of these various styles. Not to mention abbey beer, brown ale, pale ale, mild ale, cream ale, old ale, Scotch ale, barley wine, Berliner weisse, biere de garde, double bock, triple bock, eisbock, dortmunder, framboise, kriek, kruidenbier, marzen, rauchbier, wheat beer, and on it goes. A cornucopia of styles and varieties, some named for the regions where they originated, some for fermentation techniques, some for the dominant flavors.

But truth be told, many beer drinkers are not familiar with all these styles (except the true beer geeks, those denizens of the craft and microbrew worlds who are so steadfastly exploratory and experimental). A sizeable chunk of beer fans are creatures of habit, the guys and girls we grew up with who still drink and enjoy some mega-brand of frosty pale lager, perhaps selecting a green-bottled import for special occasions. Which is cool, as we all have our own palates; and think about it … there's hardly room on the leading edge for everyone. These hardworking, no-nonsense folks love a tasty pour as much as the next hophead and they're brand loyal to a fault. Not to mention good hosts. When inviting friends to dinner or a party, the question posed is, "What kind of beer does so-and-so drink?" And if so-and-so likes amber ale, you can bet there'll be amber ale awaiting. Along with their own brand, of course; they may respect your brand—but still prefer their own.

An Englishman with his legs wrapped around a pub stool (though most pubs don't have stools) would no more consider substituting a Finnish Sahti for his local draft than a Super Bowl party-goer would give up his or her favored lager for a week's worth of Belgian framboise, imperial stout or a nice, cloudy hefeweizen.

That's not to say drinkers of the pale and fizzy won't experiment. It's always fun when visiting fellow imbibers to bring along a six pack or two of something out of the ordinary. A great saison or a rare Belgian witbier is always welcome at a gathering of hops fans.

■ REAL WORLD ■

I used to visit a group of beer drinking friends who lived about a three hour drive from me. On the way out of town I would stop at an outstanding liquor store that featured the area's best selection of regional craft brews and international beers. And I always bought a mixed case, four six packs of the most obscure and unusual brews I could find. As you might imagine, my buddies looked forward to my arrival as one of the highlights of the weekend.

But if your friends are like mine: smart and wonderful people each and every one, the same thing will happen. They'll all drink and comment and enjoy, dissect and discuss and weigh the merits. And have another; ask again where you found this gem and how much it cost. But when the party's over, when the novelty has worn off and the weekend comes to an end, when everyone goes back to their daily routine, their beer choice will as well. A green-label lager drinker will always reach for a green-label lager, a lover of Mexican dark beer will stock up on Mexican dark beer. Some beer drinkers will never vary from "their brand," regardless of the situation. And yet this, my fellow admirers of John Barleycorn, is a habit best left behind as one journeys to the land of wine.

Wine drinkers, unlike the mainstream of beer and ale imbibers, are foolishly, almost recklessly experimental. They'll stick their glass out for a taste of something new, unusual or seldom seen quicker than you can slap a screw in the cork. Just mention that you picked up a great new Malbec from Argentina or a juicy little Albariño from Spain and with their very next breath you'll hear, "Well, let's give it a try." And if they like it, you can bet your bottom dollar that they'll soon be buying a few bottles, if not cases, to add to their own collections. Or at least a bottle for next Wednesday's dinner.

There is no shame among serious grape-guzzlers. Heaven forbid you should mention that you have a well-known and highly regarded wine in your possession. If you don't immediately offer to open the bottle and share your prized juice—or booty, as it is often looked upon—you'll be subject to strange, pleading looks from all the drinkers gathered around.

In your quest to know and enjoy fine wine, and an admirable quest it is, there are three elements of wino behavior that you should understand, and may also recognize in your extreme beer drinking friends:

1.) Wine drinkers, like the most radical of beer geeks, are aroma and flavor junkies. As there are literally thousands of different wines in the world, far more even than styles of beer, this always-hungry-for-the-next-bottle behavior is an evolutionary development that helps to increase the number of sniffing and tasting experiences a wine drinker can have in his or her lifetime.

2.) Wine drinking is almost never a solitary activity. Wine drinkers need to share. You'll seldom see a grape nut sitting alone at a bar nursing a great bottle of wine. It's just not much fun. Like professional athletes chest-slamming after a great play, wine drinkers revel in word-slamming about a great glass of juice (more on the wacky world of wine-speak later). Wine drinkers love to casually toss out the names and vintages of the well-known, hard-to-find wines in their possession. They crave those strange, pleading looks that imply they have something desirable; hey, it builds self- esteem. And in the end, they, too, want to open the bottle and pass it around. They want you to "ooh" and "ahh" and share in the glory of their find and the excellence of their collection.

3.) Wine is very much an accompaniment to food. Remember, we said aroma and *flavor* junkies, and that quest for taste sensation certainly extends to food. While beer is most commonly viewed as a beverage—despite the growing trend of beer and food pairing—that's sometimes refreshing, sometimes calming, sometimes thirst-quenching but essentially a beverage, wine people view their favored drink as an experience enhancer, as something not just to accompany but to improve the quality of a meal. In fact, one could make the case that most wine is consumed *with* food: as an aperitif, a course by course accompaniment, a dessert or an after-dinner conversation-stimulant. And there's no question that the right wine matched with the right food raises both to new heights.

You may already be aware of the craft brew world's interest in pairing good food and great beer. This is undoubtedly one of the most exciting areas of current beer culture. Beer and beer maker dinners are cropping up all over. Even if your beer drinking is a few sessions a month with the guys, maybe a backyard get-together with the families and a cooler of chilled something-or-other, you really should seek out a restaurant or brewery that's sponsoring a beer dinner. You'll likely have a great evening and discover some delicious new brews at the same time.

That said, not many beer drinkers (with the exceptions noted above) are likely to hunt down a specific exotic, as in not easy to find, beer to accompany the evening meal. Wine drinkers, on the other hand, live for this kind of challenge. Just tell any wino you know that you're having such and such for dinner and ask if he or she will bring along a bottle of something appropriate. Be they beginner, intermediate or advanced, you will have set off a firestorm of activity that could range from a run to the local wine shop to a call to friends with more wine knowledge than they to a look through a relevant wine book to a review of his or her cellar inventory to a further round of questioning regarding sauces to be used, anticipated side dishes, etc.

The best advice for a worthy beer drinker preparing to broach the world of wine is to stay loose. Go with the flow, be ready to experiment, and be open to new flavors and a new way of looking at what you're drinking—not that a serious beer drinker doesn't do so anyway. But don't take any of it too seriously; after all, in the end it's just fermented grape juice. And above all, avoid the noise on either side of what really shouldn't be an argument, the beer vs. wine, which is better, older, more beloved, more versatile, more this or less that, blah, blah, blah competition. It's amazing how tiresome the snobs on either side can be; they are best given a wide berth. After all, the objective here is to enjoy and have fun.

And there are plenty of great folks in both camps who approach their favored tipple in just that way.

You'll have little trouble finding a wine lover you connect with, someone who'll enjoy sharing both their wine and their knowledge, who'll be happy to assist you in navigating the terrain. You may want to go to a public tasting somewhere, perhaps at a festival or a wine shop or a restaurant in your area. Make yourself available to wine and you'll be surprised at how readily it becomes available to you.

Another point is to realize that because we're not taught to use language to describe tastes and aromas, you'll often feel as if you're not "getting it" when you drink with more practiced wine folk. I can't tell you how many times I've heard a newbie to the wine scene bemoan his or her inability to discern the nose of "sour cherry, leather and hints of orange peel" that everyone else claims to perceive and complain, pleadingly, that it just smells like … wine. Don't worry. It's just a matter of experience, of making associations in your mind. You'll begin to catch on, to understand what they claim to be smelling and tasting, sooner than you expect.

And don't try to memorize every country and every varietal and all the mass of wine lore you run across. No one—I repeat, no one—knows it all. So however knowledgeable people may appear regarding wine, there's probably more about the subject that they don't know than they do.

Wine drinkers are actually pretty cool folks. Sure, you may run into some overbearing wine geek who'll try to impress you, but there are idiots in every field (though, admittedly, wine snobs are among the worst). Just tell the overbearing clown that it's obvious he knows a lot more than you do, and you'll take the wind right out of his sails.

Give them half a chance and the bulk of wine lovers can be a lot of fun. They like to party, drink and share, and invite each other to a variety of tastings and functions where all the above takes place. Like the majority of beer drinkers, they're a gregarious group.

Grab a bottle of something and join them, or throw your own tasting party and have everyone bring along a bottle (so you can try a bunch of new wines on their nickel). You will find yourself very welcome as you move into the world of wine. And you might even be able to turn some of your new friends on to a great beer along the way. So relax, pour yourself a glass of something good and read on.

■ ■ ■ ■

The Fermentation Twins:
A Decidedly Delicious Duo

It's important, before delving further into the subject at hand, to make it clear that there is no beverage prejudice here. Wine is a fabulous drink and so too is beer. (Milk, on the other hand, is highly questionable—except for children, teens, nursing kids or calves, or anyone with a wedge of chocolate cake stuffed in their face. But then, the name of this book isn't *A Beer Drinkers' Guide To Milk,* is it?)

So let's not get hung up on the beer drinker-vs.-wine drinker thing. Didn't mean to get you all riled up with the beer drinker brand-loyalty discourse. The purpose here is to guide a group of people who usually enjoy one type of fermented beverage to the equally rich and satisfying enjoyment of another. Personally, I find them both delicious and hope you will, too, after being introduced to the ins and outs of knowing and enjoying fine wine.

■ *REAL WORLD* ■

Think back to the first sip of beer you ever had and you'll probably remember how horrible it tasted. My initial experience with the grain of the gods took place one evening in the living room of the family home. Dad was home from work at the end of a sweltering summer day and had poured himself a tall Narragansett to take the edge off. Pain in the rear that I was at the age of 3 or 4, I pestered him for a sip until he gave in.

"All right," I remember him saying. "But you may not like it."

My heart soared, for with those words, I knew I had prevailed. I stood next to him and he carefully lifted the pilsner to my lips and tipped it just enough for me to get a taste.

"Yecchhh!" What was that? Had my childish tongue deceived me? How could people sigh with such pleasure after swallowing that swill? Just to be sure, eyes rolling in my head, I asked for another sip. And doggone if the second wasn't as bad as the first.

So that's what beer tastes like. Definitely uninterested in a third go, I returned to my toy soldiers. The aftertaste, I still remember, hung with me—and was not entirely unpleasant. Even so, that experience satisfied my beer curiosity for a very long time.

My first sip of wine was some years later. I was probably all of 9 or 10. Again my father, who in truth drank very little, facilitated my introduction. He enjoyed a single small glass of red wine each evening before dinner. We were very American: a single glass before, not with, dinner, and that from a jug kept next to the potatoes under the kitchen sink.

In this case I recall the smell, rather than the taste, most distinctly. Rich and dense, vaguely fruity and very alcoholic, it wafted in great powerful waves directly up my tender young nose. Wow! What a hit. My head swirled with sensory overload and impressions unlike anything I'd ever experienced. The actual taste, by the time I got to it, was almost an afterthought. My brain was so jazzed by the aromas and "nose" of the wine that my palate could barely function. Again, I wondered how people could enjoy this stuff. But I was a bit older and had begun to suspect that perhaps grown-ups had a different "taster" than we kids. Little did I know ....

So here I am, years later, with a taste for *both* beer and wine while many, if not most, "grown-up" drinkers seem to gravitate to one beverage or the other almost exclusively. What a loss. Why shut the door on either of these luscious libations?

Deriving pleasure from both beer and wine is no different than enjoying a great dog at a summertime weenie roast and looking forward to a perfectly prepared fillet of salmon for dinner; or enjoying your favorite pair of jeans but being equally at home in a suit and tie when the occasion demands. A wine drinker who consistently turns his nose up at the offer of a good beer is a lightweight snob with no sense of adventure, while a beer drinker who won't, under any circumstance, enjoy a glass of wine is, at best, a simpleton with little hope for the future. At least that's my take.

Now that we've cleared that up, let's move on to some reasons why we might enjoy not just one or the other but, hopefully, both of these superb beverages.

The similarities between beer and wine far outweigh their differences. Both are products of fermentation; both are made in many, many styles; both appeal to our senses of sight, smell and taste; both pair wonderfully with a variety of foods; and both are legitimate options for any connoisseur of fine food and drink.

Perhaps a true appreciation is best founded on a solid understanding of just what these drinks really are and how they come to be, so why not start with a quick refresher in the fine and ancient art of beer-making? This should also be helpful to any stray wine drinkers who might be joining us.

■ *TECHNICAL DRIVEL* ■

It all starts with grain. Most commonly barley, but wheat, rye, oats and even rice can be used (yes, Martha, sake is actually rice beer, not rice wine). Grains are loaded with starch that first has to be converted to sugar. The process begins with "malting." Grains are soaked in water to start germination, just as you would germinate any seeds or cuttings. As the sprouts begin to grow and break through the grain husk, nature does a rather remarkable thing: enzymes emerge within the grain for the purpose of converting the starch into sugar to feed the growing sprout. At this point the grain is heated in an oven or kiln to stop the process, lest the starch be converted to sugar and consumed by the hungry young plant before the brewer can make use of it.

Next the grain is milled—or broken apart—and dropped into a copper or stainless steel vessel, the mash tun, to begin the process of "mashing." Hot water is added and the mixture is heated and steeped, creating a thin gruel, the "mash." Those enzymes are now back in business and get to work converting the starches to sugar, a process known as "saccharification." When complete, the resulting "wort" or sugar water, is transferred to a brew kettle and set to boiling.

During the boil, the third ingredient (malted barley and water being the first two) is added to the mix. This critical element is hops, the flower of the hop vine, which contains acids that give beer its characteristic bitterness, as well as adding flavor and aroma. There are numerous varieties of hops, and each provides beer with a slightly different profile.

After an hour or two of boiling (depending on the type of beer being brewed) the wort is cooled and pumped into a fermentation tank. It is here where the final ingredient, yeast, is added and the actual fermentation begins. Yeast is a single-cell organism that consumes sugar and converts it to alcohol and carbon dioxide. Yeast, like hops, comes in many varieties, some of which are used to make bread or other foods (and of course, wine) and each of which adds its own flavor.

Primary fermentation takes from three to seven days. The beer may undergo a secondary fermentation wherein the CO_2 that's produced naturally carbonates the beer. Once fermentation is complete the beer is filtered and pumped to a stainless steel tank for a period of R&R, officially known as conditioning. It's held in cold storage in this tank for a few days (for ales) or weeks or months (for lagers) as the beer takes final shape. From here it's usually fined, filtered, bottled and shipped to your favorite store or pub.

The wine drinkers who have been eavesdropping will find much of this process to be quite familiar. Wine, of course, begins with grapes, not grains. Literally thousands of grape varieties are used to make wine, although most commercially available wine is produced from only a few dozen types (unless you're fortunate enough to live in Italy, where wine is made from close to a thousand distinct varieties of grape).

While much of the two processes are similar, the actual growing of the grape has a huge effect on the quality and flavors of the resulting wine, much more so than the growing conditions of barley or hops affect the beer made from them.

But before we get into the nuances of winegrowing, let's take a look at winemaking. After being picked, grapes are transported to the winery. Often, the grapes are de-stemmed, either by hand or by machine, before being crushed. If a white wine is being made, the grape juice is immediately separated from the skins and seeds and transferred to a stainless steel fermenting tank.

If red wine is in the making, the juice is allowed to sit on the skins for anywhere from a few hours to a few weeks, a step called "maceration." It's the skins that contribute the color to a red wine, since the juice from most grapes, red or white, is actually clear. Leaving the juice on the skins and seeds also allows "tannins" to leach into the mixture. And it's those tannins that give red wine its structure, improve its ability to age and leave you with that dry, "puckery," taste in the mouth. In most instances, a second crushing, or "pressing," will take place to remove all the juice from the grapes and skins.

Fermentation of wine, just like fermentation of beer, occurs when yeasts convert sugar into alcohol. But since grape juice already contains sugar, there is no need to first go through the malting or saccharification steps necessary in beer-making. In this regard, the wine-making process is a bit simpler, or at least involves fewer steps. And while yeasts are added to the crushed juice to begin fermentation, there are also naturally occurring yeasts already present on the skins of the grapes.

In fact, grapes are the perfect little package: sugary juice on the inside, wild yeast on the outside. Just crush them to break the skins—and wait for wine to happen!

Almost. While some traditional winemakers, especially in parts of Europe, rely primarily on the indigenous, or "wild," yeasts found not only on grapes but throughout their wineries and vineyards, many winemakers add various other strains of yeast that, as with beer, affect the flavors and texture of the resulting product. In fact, the yeast species Saccharomyces cerevisiae is the most important for both wine and beer (especially ale) production. Added strains keep the fermentation progressing as heat and alcohol levels rise, add complexity to the flavors, and help to avoid the funky odors that natural yeasts can at times produce.

One thing winemakers don't need to concern themselves with, however, is adjuncts. (For you wine geeks reading along, adjuncts are any additional grains, such as rice, corn or rye, or syrups, fruits or flavorings used in brewing, either to reduce cost or to enhance the taste of the finished product.) Wine is strictly grape juice transformed. There may a bit of sulphur to prevent spoilage or in some countries the addition of sugar to increase body and alcohol, but fine wine is about the grapes: their variety, their ripeness, and their concentration of flavors.

> **All this talk of fermentation is making me thirsty.**
> **It's close to lunchtime and I have bottles of Duvel Belgian**
> **and Abita Turbodog, one of my longtime faves,**
> **in the reefer—not to mention my entire wine cellar.**
> **Oh, the choices ...**

Most fermentation takes place in steel tanks, sometimes in oak casks or barrels, and a surprising amount of wine is still fermented in lined concrete vats. In any case, the sugars are converted to alcohol until all the sugar is gone or all the yeast is used up. With white wines, a second fermentation may be allowed that converts sharp-tasting malic acid into softer lactic acid. Some winemakers, however, prefer the cleaner, purer flavors of the primary fermentation and don't make use of malolactic fermentation at all.

Once fermentation is complete, the dead yeast cells and remaining solids are allowed to sink slowly to the bottom of the vessel. The newly fermented wine is then transferred to either oak barrels or large casks for aging. Whites may be filtered and bottled immediately or aged for as much a year in oak and then bottled. Reds are usually aged longer and undergo additional racking (pumping or siphoning the wine off the accumulated solids in the bottom of the barrel) for anywhere from six months to four years before bottling.

While there are myriad variations, additional considerations and subtleties to either process, these big-picture explanations make it easy to see how similar beer-making and winemaking are. In both cases a natural product, whether grape or grain, provides starch and sugar and inherent flavors; the addition of yeast converts the sugars to alcohol and enhances the flavors (with a little assist from the hops when making beer), giving us a drink worthy of good times and great enjoyment.

Now that we've discussed winemaking (viniculture), it's important to get a little dirt under the fingernails and turn our attention to grape growing (viticulture). What happens in the winery is immensely important, but regardless of the skill and experience of the winemaker, no great wine is made without having first-rate fruit to work with. Among wine lovers and producers alike, it's commonly said that great wine is made in the vineyard.

Grape vines in their native state are climbers. As recently as a few decades ago it wasn't unusual for vines in remote parts of Italy and Europe to grow up and around trees, like any other climbing vine. Harvesting meant propping a wooden ladder against the trunk and climbing up to pick the bunches. Taking the vines out of the woodlands and planting them where it's easier to control their development and surroundings is the first step to improving quality. Of course, nothing is easy. Where best to plant them? Well, duh, how about where the soil is fertile and the water plentiful?

Wrong, Grasshopper! That would be the worse place to plant. Vines, like rabbits and teenagers, just want to reproduce, to guarantee survival of the species. In the case of *Vitis vinifera*, the vine responsible for 99% of all fine wine grapes, rich soil and an abundance of water mean the plant will explode with foliage and shoots and tendrils. A happy plant. But not one overly concerned with producing exceptional grapes. On the other hand, make conditions a little tougher, plant that vine in rocky or sandy conditions where nothing else wants to grow, where water is sparse and nutrients hard to find, and something quite interesting takes place. The vine thinks (go with me on this one) *Hey, this is no place to raise a tender young shoot. It's time to move the family.* This, in the world of rooted plants means generating high-grade seeds to be eaten and dropped or excreted elsewhere by birds and other of nature's helpful critters.

Now, without water or good soil the vine's feeling some stress. And so the quality of the grapes goes up as more of the plant's resources are redirected from leaves and tendrils to the next generation. In fact, prune back a bunch of leaves and clip off half the grape clusters and things really get interesting. The vine's resources, including all those stored sugars from photosynthesis, are fed to the remaining grapes, meaning that with fewer of them competing, each cluster gets more of the good stuff. Grape sugars intensify, anthocyanins and polyphenols (the color, flavor and aroma elements) ratchet up and the result is a higher quality grape that will produce a richer, more complex wine.

The trick is to get all this done in the vineyard, at the right time and in the right proportions without being overly harsh. Too many leaves removed and the vine can't synthesize adequate nutrients and the grapes themselves may get sunburned, too few removed and the grapes impart a green, weedy taste to the wine and may not reach full maturity, and various molds and diseases find places to hide in and among the canopy of leaves. If grape clusters are going to be lopped off (green harvested) to enrich the final crop, it can't be done too early or too late. And what's right one year can be very different the next with changes in the amount of rainfall and cloud cover. Something as simple as having more wind one year or a spell of abnormally warm nights shortly before harvest can significantly alter procedures in the winemaking.

Every day brings another dozen decisions. This is very hands-on farming. Do we plant cover crops between rows to give the vines some competition for water and nutrients in areas that might be too fertile? Do we prune the vines in this style or that to have just the right leaf area and arrangement in the canopy? Are the nights staying cool enough to maintain the desired acid levels? If not, will we have to pick the grapes earlier? Or do we let the grapes hang longer to build more sugar? Should we water now or hold off for a few more days?

> **The French have no word for winemaker, and refer instead to the *vigneron*, meaning the wine grower. Their vocabulary says much.**

The ideal scenario is to have everything in the vineyard come together in glorious harmony. The grapes' acid and sugar levels reach perfect balance at the exact moment when its seeds and skins are fully ripe. This, as discussed, is dependent on many factors including rain and wind and temperature and sunshine and bugs and pests and the myriad daily decisions made by the man or woman in charge. Some regions are fortunate to have climactic and *terroir* conditions that cooperate with this objective. Others are not. Which makes a good vintage especially welcome.

So the next time you pull a cork or twist a screwcap, give a moment's thought to what it takes to create that delicious mouthful of nature's bounty you're about to enjoy. Be it red, white, rosé or sparkling, raise your glass in appreciation to all the world's great winemakers and grape growers. And while we're at it, cheers to the brew masters, too; thanks for all those great glasses of amber, red and brown. Here, here!

■ ■ ■ ■

3

Embrace Your Inner Wino:
Thoughts on What To Drink When

Instead of automatically reaching for a beer, give some thought to the great variety of fine wines able to more than satisfy your cravings at any given time, in any given situation. Why not consider a gorgeous glass of juice, while remembering a few critical differences?

First Consideration: Glass for glass, wine packs a lot more punch than beer. These days the average alcohol level of wine is close to 14%, more than twice the 6%, give or take, of most beer. Yes, ales, certain specialty beers and a number of craft brews can be quite a bit higher, just as some sweet or fizzy wines can be lower, some as low as 5%. But overall, you should realize that wine is made for savoring, not guzzling. There's no need to hammer a glass of fine wine, because the longer you hold off and the longer it sits in your glass, the better it gets.

Second Consideration: Wine, with a few exceptions, likes to relax, to take in the air, to get out of the bottle and stretch a little, maybe even catch a short nap in your glass before you suck it all down.

■ *REAL WORLD* ■

One of the drinking world's dirty little secrets, well known to just about any hop head is that, with a few particular exceptions, the most delicious swallow of beer is the first. Decidedly. The second may be near-great, the third terrific, but they've all started the big, slow slide from perfection. By the time you reach the bottom of the mug or bottle, you just want it gone so you can order another and begin with that fantastic first sip all over again. Wine is just the opposite, its first sip is often tight, still coming to, waking up from a long oxygen-deprived rest in the bottle.

Why do you think beer drinkers start with that big take-it-a-third-of-the-way-down swallow when served? Then a little nursing until there's only a big slug left ... at which time the vessel in question is upended, drained, and slammed onto the bar for a refill.

In contrast, watch a wine drinker sip his or her way through a glass of exceedingly good vino. There are oohs and aahs of anticipation; there's discourse and discussion and entire conversations about the evolution—in the glass—of the beverage being enjoyed. And as the end approaches, the ratio of sniffing to swallowing goes up dramatically. Why? Because with each passing minute the wine interacts with oxygen and "opens up," getting noticeably better. New aromas and complexities reach out from the glass, triggering waves of pleasure and reminiscence. The wine is stretching, coming fully to life, and the end of these, its best moments, is put off for as long as possible.

So with that beautiful glass of wine, sip and swirl and fully enjoy each and every swallow, stifling your amazement that it opens up and offers greater complexity and enjoyment as you work your way from top to bottom. Wine drinkers know the last mouthful is always the best. And often when they've gone through a bottle of really good stuff too quickly, you'll hear, "Man, oh man, what a beautiful wine. But doggone, we drank it too fast; that last swallow was fan-damn-tastic!"

Third Consideration: Get the temperature right. This is more important than you may think and has a major impact on the way a wine tastes and smells. There's a tendency to drink white wines too cold and reds too warm. This really makes a difference in your physiological response, and therefore *in your enjoyment,* of what's in the glass. If you're spending your money, why not do all you can to maximize your pleasure?

White wine should be served in the neighborhood of 45 to 55ºF (7 to 13ºC), not at straight-from-the-reefer temps of 38 to 40º F or less. If you have a bottle chilling behind the milk and the juice, pull it out a good half-hour before you serve it.

I can hear some drinkers yelling at me for this one. "It should be colder," they're saying. "Crisp. Right from the refrigerator is perfect." Well, pardon me while I disagree. Those super cold temps may be fine for a light-bodied lager, but honestly, would you serve an imperial stout that chilly? Of course not, and you shouldn't serve a good white wine that cold either. If you do, the aromas, the nuances, the gorgeous hints of peach and pear, of apple and fig and tropical fruit, the subtle notes of minerality will all be lost. Cold shuts wine down. Many sommeliers assessing wines for possible inclusion on wine lists won't even try wines that are too low in temperature. Why? Because you can't smell or taste what's in the glass.

So pry the ice cubes out of your mouth. If you need super cold to cool you down and provide refreshment on a hot day, try some iced tea or that frosty lager. Or if you must, crank up the air conditioning. But if you're sitting by the pool whiling away a leisurely afternoon or having a before-dinner glass to whet your appetite or enjoying a course of light, fresh food, allow the wine to participate. Your palate will thank me.

25

Reds are best served in the 55-65°F (13-18°C) range, on the cooler end for lighter reds like Chiantis and Beaujolais, and on the warmer end for heavier reds like Cabernet and Syrah. And yes, I've heard all that "room-temperature" talk—and I agree. So if you live in a stone farmhouse in rural France, heated only by a stove or fireplace, and you're climbing up from the cellar with a bottle to accompany your cassoulet on a breezy autumn's eve, by all means serve it at room temperature. Remember, that's where the little nugget about room temperature originated, and where it's appropriate.

■ *TECHNICAL DRIVEL* ■

Most of what we experience when we enjoy the flavor of wine or beer enters our brains by way of what's called the retro-nasal cavity, and a compact, highly sensitive group of cells, the olfactory epithelium, located more or less at the base of our sinuses, high up in our nasal cavity where it connects with the upper reaches of our throat.

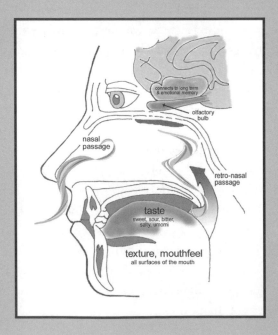

The tongue and inside of the mouth are the sites of our taste buds, which are sensitive to sweet, sour, salt, bitter and umami—and nothing more. Everything else that we consider "taste" is actually a chemical reaction that occurs in the retro-nasal cavity and olfactory epithelium: all those complex identifiable flavors of berries and chocolate and licorice and kiwi and leather and coffee and lychee and ... well, you get the point.

The bulk of those flavors and aromas are carried from a glass of wine to our retro-nasal cavity by means of volatile compounds—i.e., compounds that evaporate quickly. Unfortunately, when a substance is cooled below a specific threshold, that evaporation is greatly reduced. Meaning that if we drink wine that's too cold, we simply fail to receive or recognize the volatile compounds that give wine much of its flavor and aroma. Hence drinking whites that are overly chilled equals no taste.

The whole volatile thing is why wine drinkers swirl their glasses; coating the inside of a wine glass with a very thin layer of wine allows it to evaporate quickly and transmit the wine's characteristics to your brain— where it can truly be enjoyed.

At the same time, red wines served too warm will throw off so much alcohol, a highly volatile substance, that it overpowers everything else. The wine will be harsh and hot and all its beauty hidden behind the alcohol. This is a common problem in restaurants, which tend to serve red wines much too warm. When the bottle you've selected is presented for your approval, put a hand on it, feel it and be sure it's cool to the touch. If not, ask your server to stick it in an ice bucket for five or ten minutes. I do this often and the wine is always better for it. In the U.S. especially, we tend to serve white wines much too cold and reds much too warm. You'll be delighted with the improvement that even five or ten minutes of temperature adjustment will bring to your meal.

So take heed. The following are suggestions to assist in the development of a more wine-centric perspective on those events and situations that you usually respond to with a bottle opener. It's time now to think beyond the church key and arm yourself with a good corkscrew.

THE SCENE ... #1

Sitting around the TV, with or without friends, watching the game and munching on chips and barbeque (a nice touch, the barbeque).

The beer: A good amber ale or a quality Mexican, i.e., Vienna-style, lager. Hey, c'mon, this kind of drinking is as basic as it gets—you're not still swallowing that flavorless, mass-produced pony p_ _ _, are you? Look, if you have to drink an American-style lager, at least find something with *Pilsner* or *Dortmunder* in the name; you'll know it will be a classic lager but much higher up in the quality department. They're not pricey and they're easy to find.

The wine: Zinfandel. Simple. Hearty with a hidden touch of sweetness to complement the barbeque and balance the saltiness of the chips. And enough alcohol that you can really get into rooting for the home team. (By the way, we're talking *red* Zinfandel here, just in case ...)

THE SCENE ... #2

Your new girlfriend's brothers have all come over to check you out on the pretense of dropping her off and asking if you'd like to go hunting with them next week.

The beer: Irish stout, duh.

The wine: A young Brunello di Montalcino. You hate to "waste" the money, but sometimes you just have to make a point. This one will rock 'em. Delicious but way too big for their lager heads. Will quite possibly bowl them over, especially if they see the price tag. You'll gain major respect.

THE SCENE ... #3

A nice restaurant with a decent beer selection, you and the squeeze having dinner with another couple or two.

The beer: Trappist ale or maybe a British bitter. Tastes great and exotic enough to make you look like someone who knows his or her stuff.

The wine: Pinot Noir, a good one. Goes moderately well with whatever food anyone's ordering and has a big "cool" factor. At least this week. Try for something from California if your group is young and still chews a lot of gum, from Oregon if they're a little classier, or from Burgundy if old people or Europeans are involved and you have too much money and would like to give some of it away.

THE SCENE ... #4

Home, the living room (or a restaurant if you're shallower than it first appeared), breaking up with the significant other before he or she breaks up with you.

The beer: Dortmunder Export (you'll have to look to find one but, hey, this scene is all about overcoming). Anyway, the choice is classy, shows maturity and a modicum of sophistication—which in theory should ease the pain and help the about-to-be-dumped appreciate the good times you've had together—but with enough oomph to get you through the drama.

The wine: Sherry. Dry. A fino or a manzanilla. Definitely an acquired taste. He or she will think maybe the two of you are on different wavelengths after all.

THE SCENE ... #5

Out to dinner with the boss and important clients and the sales team. The boss hands you the wine list—"Here you go, Johnson. I understand you're a wine drinker." Formerly a sweaty-palms moment, right?

The beer: Not an option. Didn't you read the scene?

The wine: Cabernet Sauvignon. Something near the borderline of too expensive. California, or if you're lucky enough to find it on the list, Washington State. The good quality stuff is good quality. Powerful and lip-smacking. It can never be a bad choice—unless everyone orders the fish with lemon sauce. In which case you tell the server he or she misunderstood; you ordered the Sauvignon Blanc, the one from the Loire, right here, at the top of the list, the Sancerre. (Nice comeback—not the perfect match, but the schlepps from sales will never know, and the boss will be impressed that you can even pronounce *Sancerre.* By the way, it's *sahn-sair.*)

THE SCENE ... #6

That aforementioned hot summer afternoon when you've just finished mowing the lawn and weeding the flowers or the vegetable garden.

The beer: Ha! You thought I was going to fall for that you-might-as-well-have-that-frosty-can-now cop-out, didn't you? Not a chance. Sure, that might quench your thirst, but so would a glass of water. Instead, treat yourself to a weissbier or a hefeweizen. These wheat beers are best served cold, though not ice-cold, and are incredibly refreshing. They will definitely restore you, and you won't feel like you swallowed a balloon afterward, as you would with that almost frozen can of you-know-what.

By the way, that big belch? Probably comes from sucking your suds on the way too chilly side of "Holy brewmeister, that's one cold ale!" In fact, the colder the beer, the worse things get. When beer is chilled, the carbon dioxide contracts and is less active—until it hits your stomach and starts warming up. Then the carbonation gets all jazzed up, expands, and bloats your gut. And you know the rest of the story.

The wine: Forget it. This is about high-volume fluid replenishment. Have the beer.

THE SCENE ... #7

Girls'—guys'—night out. Dinner at the group's favorite restaurant before heading to the local hot spot. The girls are dishing about work and men; the guys are talking shop and sports and waiting for the right moment to start dishing about women.

The beer: For the girls, unlikely. Let's be real—the ladies are going for Cosmos or martinis, maybe Sex on the Beach. Call me names if you like, but the odds for suds here are slim to ain't gonna happen.

The beer: For the guys, the quick grab would be something green and Dutch, but why not sing out for a round of top-notch amber ale or, if it's available, a great altbier from Düsseldorf, something malty with a nice hits of hops.

The wine: For the ladies, no way we'll give the nod to a flabby Merlot or some watery Pinot Grigio. Instead, how about a Spanish Albariño, on everyone's wine list, finally, or a Greek Nemea, showcasing the lovely, soft red variety Agiorítiko.

The wine: For the gentlemen, time to show your chops, wouldn't you think? A five- to eight-year-old Bordeaux, still showing some great tannins, enough fruit to keep the boys engaged, and leather and tobacco to complement that juicy marbled steak. Or a Muscadet Sèvre et Maine from the mouth of the Loire if it's a particularly tough crowd, a bunch of coastal wise-guys who like to suck down a couple dozen oysters before moving on to the main event. (Wise-guys with a palate—the easiest of all to manipulate into the pleasures of the grape.)

AND FINALLY, THE SCENE ... #8

The summer cookout, a dozen or more good friends answering your invitation to a day of fun, frolic, burgers, dogs, barbeque chicken, shrimp on the barbie and those exotic sausages you found at the downtown meat market.

The beer: Forget everyone's favorite. This is the perfect opportunity to expand horizons. Fill a big cooler, or two, with ice and stuff them full of a selection of great craft brews: fruit beers, wheat beers, IPAs, pilsners, pale ales, and anything and everything you know you should have tried but haven't had the chance to yet. You'll give them a great experience and create some buzz. And save me a sausage, I might be a little late.

The wine: Hope you've got another cooler. Some dry Provencal rosé, a great—and inexpensive—Rhone white, a good unoaked Chardonnay and some delicious New Zealand Sauvignon Blanc. And for the sausage eaters, a South African Shiraz, a hearty, Grenache-based Vacqueyras, and if you're really "the man" a Lagrein Riserva from northern Italy.

But these are just suggestions. If beer has been your beverage of choice, the point is to enlarge your liquor vocabulary. Try this and try that—wine-wise, that is—and reach your own conclusions.

You might really enjoy a Chilean cab with fried chicken or a white Rioja with pepperoni pizza. All of which is great. The objective is to begin appreciating the power and glory and diversity of this sumptuous class of drink. Drink red wine with fish and whites with meat and see what happens. We all have our own quirky tastes and we all respond a little differently to various stimuli. There'll be time enough to develop "expertise"; the first step is simply to expose yourself to the richness of flavors and textures and aromas that are the hallmark of good wines everywhere.

■ ■ ■ ■

4
Enough Jawboning, Let's Drink: Finally, It's Time for Tasting

Let's quit fooling around and get down to it.

It's time to put the cards on the table and the juice in the glass. All this jabbering won't reveal half as much about the charms and gusto of good wine as will a single sip. And right here, at the beginning, is the perfect time to let you in on the tasting secrets that make wine even more enjoyable.

Wine tasting is like anything else: the more you know about what you're doing, the more you'll get out of it. Think of watching baseball with a friend from another country who's not familiar with the national sport. He or she may recognize the athleticism of an outstanding play, but will never see the strategies or subtleties, or get nearly the pleasure from the game that you will. When that suicide squeeze in the bottom of the ninth makes the crowd go wild, he'll be slow to his feet and not really understand what all the commotion is about.

But let's not get carried away. Tasting wine isn't advanced physics. If you know how to drink, you know how to taste. The only difference with wine is that you need to do it a little more slowly and to pay a little more attention. For example, before you suck it down, take a look at what's in your glass. Wine (like beer) is a beautiful thing, literally, so take a minute to really look at it, to think about and describe the color, to notice if the wine is crystal clear, cloudy, or kind of bubbly. See? Not a big deal. But that kind of attention is the key to formal wine tasting.

It's not unlike formal beer tasting, although most structured beer evaluation is done as part of a handful of major events and competitions, like the Great American Beer Festival or the National Homebrew Competition. Wine drinkers, however, even relatively casual ones, love to put pen to paper and go through the drill of scoring and assessing what's in the glass. It's been my experience that barleycorn drinkers, some quite knowledgeable about everything from yeast to hops to various international styles, are more prone to give their brew an appreciative but quick look-see, a passing sniff and then down the hatch.

■ TECHNICAL DRIVEL ■

If you're turning a more critical eye to the suds in your mug, you'll probably begin with color, or degrees SRM (standard reference method), as the American Society of Brewing Chemists terms it. This color scale ranges from pale straw—perhaps 1.5 degrees SRM, as found in light American lager—to as high as 80 degrees SRM, as found in a near-black Imperial stout.

To get you oriented, a witbier might run from pale straw at 2° SRM to pale gold around 4° SRM; an Abbey Tripel from 3.6° to 6° SRM, or deep gold; an IPA from 6° to 12° or 14° SRM, essentially a medium amber; a doppelbock from 15° SRM all the way to brown at 24° SRM; and an Irish stout would hover between 30° and 40° SRM.

In any case, drinking is done for pleasure; tasting is done for assessment. Perhaps to determine if a wine is worth its price or decide if you want to buy some to take home, or if you just want to learn about the various grape varietals and how they differ from place to place or how specific winemaking techniques alter the finished product. Actually, tasting like a pro is simpler than you might imagine; as mentioned, it follows the natural steps we take in drinking any beverage. While you can't expect to learn as much at first as a wine professional does when tasting, you can quickly become comfortable with the process and, in so doing, increase your level of knowledge and degree of pleasure.

■ ■ ■

There is a logical, set progression to tasting wine for the purpose of evaluation. Tasters start by ...

1.) gathering information about the wine in question, information that's accumulated through the senses of sight, smell, taste and feel. As these impressions are acquired it's helpful to write them down, both to reinforce your objectivity and to have a record for future reference. Once the information is gathered, tasters move on to ...

2.) analyzing it. In other words, figuring out what the impressions—i.e., the assembled information—says about the wine. At first this means understanding whether a particular characteristic is good or bad and to what degree. When you've become more experienced, this same set of information can tell you what grape or grapes were used, what climate they were grown in, what country and maybe what region the wine is from, its age and general condition, and even the techniques of the winemaker. After you've gathered and analyzed all this, you'll find yourself almost automatically ...

3.)   determining if the wine is good or bad, so-so or outstanding, well made or poorly made, problematic or nearly perfect.

On one hand, it's fairly straightforward: gather the information, assess the information you've gathered, and make a determination. On the other hand, it's not really done in three distinct steps but as a fluid process. A taster gathers a bit of info and makes a preliminary evaluation of what that info says, then gathers another piece of information, assesses it, and relates it back to the first impression. And so on until a final picture emerges and a reasonable conclusion can be reached.

Instead of just telling you that color, clarity, flavors, etc. provide clues to what's in your glass, what the varietal is, where it might be from and so on, the next section will spell out the specifics so you can put all your observations and impressions to good use.

THE PROCESS: PART 1—SEE

Pour a couple inches of the wine to be tasted into a stemmed wine glass with a tulip-shaped, tapered bowl. Now look at it. Closely. In good light. Is the wine clear or hazy? Still or bubbly? Is it red or white? All pretty basic. So let's sharpen our focus a bit, though all we need do at first is learn to observe. The interpretation of what we see, smell, taste and feel comes later.

If the wine is clear, is it star-bright or just clear? If it's hazy, is there a general cloudiness, or do you see discernable particles floating in it? Is it bubbly? If you're looking at Champagne or another type of sparkling wine, it had better be, but if you're looking at a regular wine—i.e., a "still" or table wine—anything more than a few bubbles around the rim that dissipate quickly should be noted.

As to color, we want to look both at the hue—a fancy term for the color itself, be it purple/red, ruby, brick, pale yellow, yellow or gold—and at the intensity or depth of color. This is best done by tilting the glass at a forty-five-degree angle and looking down into the wine against a well-lighted white background. It's pretty tough (read: impossible) to judge color against a dark, colored, or poorly lighted background. So if you're having dinner in a dark and cozy supper club, you'd best leave the visual wine judging to another time and place—and rest your gaze instead on that lovely creature sitting across the table from you.

> *"Come, my dear. One more glass,*
> *to celebrate your beauty."*

But after your night of revelry, when you're ready to get back to the business of tasting, pick your glass up by the stem, hold it at a forty-five-degree angle over a white background and decide what color the wine is. Remember, begin by looking down into the center of the wine, and then move your focus to the edge, where the color will start to become either lighter or darker. What color is it? How dark is it? How much shift in color is there from the center to the rim?

The color will give you clues to the varietal and, at least as far as white wines are concerned, some idea about the winemaking process. The depth of color will provide further information concerning the kind of grapes in your glass, and the color of the rim, along with its difference from the color in the center, will provide hints to the wine's age.

THE PROCESS: PART 2—SNIFF

Now, on to the nose. Or put more clearly, what does the wine smell like? This step is a little more complicated than just looking at the wine. When smelling, or "nosing," a wine, you're seeking similarities to known aromas. Sometimes—actually quite often when you're just beginning—you'll recognize a smell from somewhere in your past. It's there in your memory bank but you can't put a finger on exactly what it is.

After a minute or two you may realize that it's the smell of your mother's fresh-baked blueberry pie, something you haven't smelled in years. Or maybe it's the scent of the wild strawberries that grew outside your family's vacation cabin in the mountains. Or the rich, wonderful smell of the empty cigar boxes your grandfather gave you to store your childhood treasures in. It might be the aroma of freshly cut grass or a particular fruit or flower or some food that you loved growing up.

Our sense of smell triggers strong associations, and it sometimes takes a few minutes to identify these memories, especially when they're coming from a glass of wine.

Technique is important as well. First, just raise the glass to your nose and inhale. Pretty simple. But now comes Lesson 1 in "Strange Wine Behavior": swirling. The purpose of swirling wine (see Technical Drivel, Chapter 3) is not to create lift and levitate from your seat or to strengthen the wrists and reverse carpal tunnel syndrome. Rather, it's intended to let you smell the wine better, or, in modified wine-speak, to enhance your appreciation of the aromas and bouquet.

By swirling, you coat the inside of the glass with a very thin layer of wine, only a few molecules thick. This layer evaporates quickly, allowing any sniffing nose that happens to be in the vicinity to get an immediate and direct whiff of the wine's volatile compounds (known scientifically as esters and aldehydes), the chemical structures that our brain interprets as smells. So while there are no actual raspberries in your glass, the same volatile compounds that are found in a particular fruit may also be present in a particular type of wine; hence the scent of raspberries in your Tempranillo.

■ *TECHNIQUE* ■

Set your glass on a table or other flat surface and begin moving it in a counterclockwise, circular pattern. As you increase speed, the wine will rise higher in the glass, coating the inside of the bowl. Your glass shouldn't be more than about a third full or the wine will spill over. This, in fact, is the main reason a proper pour of wine is never more than 25% or 30% of the glass.

Now raise the glass to your nose—don't be afraid to stick the old honker right in there—and take a series of short, sharp sniffs. Focus. Let the aromas fill your nasal cavity. Then give your glass another swirl and do it all over again.

For best results, don't use long, deep inhalations. For some reason these seem to tire the nose and lessen your ability to discern subtle differences in aromas. Just watch a cat or dog that's caught the scent of something interesting. It uses a series of small, quick sniffs to gather information. You'll never see Fido rear up on his hind legs and snort down a big, drawn out noseful of air to figure out what that intriguing aroma might be.

With practice, you'll be able to swirl with the best of them without even setting your glass on a table, though this is hardly important. What is important is to realize that you'll get more information about a wine from your sense of smell than you will from either seeing or even tasting it. So take your time here. Don't rush. Get all the clues you can about a wine before you taste it. In short order, you will begin to develop a new sensitivity to scents and aromas that has probably lain dormant for a long time (this will also make it much more enjoyable when you actually do stop to smell the roses).

"Tears" or "legs" are formed as the alcohol in that thin layer of wine begins to evaporate and the remaining liquid starts its slow descent down the inside of the glass, giving us one last visual clue to consider. A wine with greater viscosity—i.e., with more pronounced "legs"—is generally a fuller-bodied wine with a higher alcohol content. Light-bodied and/or low-alcohol wines tend not to display well-defined streams but rather to show thin areas of moisture with some minor tearing on the inside of the glass.

THE PROCESS: PART 3—SIP

Now that you've seen and smelled, it's time to taste. Finally. By this point you've earned the right to taste and enjoy. So do. Take a good, healthy swig and swish it all around your mouth. Make note of the very first flavors and sensations as the wine enters your mouth.

Is it tart? Just slightly, not at all, or very much so? This is the wine's acidity. It's important that a wine have good acidity or it will taste flat and lifeless. Acidity helps to cleanse and refresh our palates. It stimulates the taste buds and improves flavors, the same effect we're looking for when we squeeze lemon onto a piece of fish or into a glass of iced tea. The flip side, of course, is too much acidity, as when the lemonade is so tart we need to stir in more sugar to bring the flavors into balance.

Next we assess the sensation of sweetness. Is the wine sweet or dry (meaning without sweetness)? You may perceive rich fruit flavors in a wine and mistake that for sweetness, even in a dry wine. *Sweetness* here refers to "residual," or leftover, sugar that remains after the wine is fermented. This may be due to the wine's style, as in German Rieslings or—excuse me, Bacchus—white Zinfandel. Or it may go hand in hand with a high-alcohol wine like many California red Zinfandels.

Hold the wine in your mouth for a few seconds while it warms to body temperature. This allows the heavier volatile compounds to begin evaporating, which enhances your taste impressions. Don't just guzzle and swallow. This isn't lemonade, it's wine. Try to coat every nook and cranny of your mouth; chew the wine if you have to. This is wine tasting. No worry about being polite here. Just be sure the wine comes into contact with your entire mouth: tongue, gums, roof, cheeks, everything.

Remember the old saw about taste sensitivity? You taste sweet only on the tip of your tongue and sour only on the sides and so on? Well, as it turns out, no one ever told our taste buds about that. Most of them, sneaky devils, have receptors that can detect all four ... er, well, now there are five, as we've come to realize that umami, or savoriness, is a taste in itself, in addition to sweet, sour, salt and bitter. They may be more receptive to sweetness, for example, at the tip of the tongue, but even there our taste buds are registering all the taste categories. And they're located just about everywhere. Besides the tongue, we have taste buds on the insides of our cheeks, on the soft palate, or roof of our mouths, even on our tonsils!

While people have different sensitivities to various taste components, meaning some people are able to detect smaller amounts of a particular taste than other people are, it has much less to do with where on the tongue or in the mouth they're tasting.

So coat your entire mouth. Give yourself a chance to get every bit of taste you can. You'll see some serious winos who go beyond that. They'll slurp and gurgle and suck air in over their tongues, doing their best Hannibal Lecter impersonations before they swallow, all in an effort to maximize the experience and nuances of taste.

Sounds kinda weird. And it looks pretty odd, too. Which brings us to Lesson 2 in "Strange Wine Behavior": slurping and sucking. If you think about it, these tasters are utilizing their mouths the way we use wine glasses when we swirl. By coating their palates with the wine being evaluated and then drawing a current of air over its surface, they're speeding up evaporation and increasing the release of the volatile compounds.

■ TECHNICAL DRIVEL ■

Once the inner surfaces of the mouth are coated with wine and the taste receptors have gotten to work, drawing air in and over the tongue evaporates the wine and sends all those chemical compounds we talked about earlier rushing up to the olfactory reception center at the base of the brain.

This is where all scents and aromas head when we smell or sniff anything. The same processing center that reminded you of Mom's blueberry pie. The most direct route is via the nostrils, but the esters and aldehydes travel throughout our sinus cavities as well. And since taste buds, though they may be everywhere, perceive only sweet, sour, bitter, salt and umami, it's really the retro-nasal cavity, to use the technical term, that creates the complex flavor sensations we think of as taste.

The old-standby proof of this is to pinch your nostrils shut so that you inhale no aromas and try a few bites of food. It will have little or no flavor. You probably won't be able to tell an apple from a potato, just as you can't taste much when you have a cold and your sinus cavities are stopped up.

Now try to feel the weight and the alcohol of the wine, two tactile sensations to be aware of. Wine drinkers refer to weight, to the viscosity and fullness of a wine in the mouth, as the wine's "body" and identify it as being light-, medium- or full-bodied. The best approximation I've heard for this is that the feel, the weight, of skim milk in your mouth is light-bodied, 2% milk feels medium-bodied and whole milk, perhaps with a touch of cream, is full-bodied. In any case, the body of the wine is definitely part of the assessment, as it, too, reveals more of the wine's secrets.

A higher alcohol level, along with greater extract (as found in deeply colored reds and wood-aged wines), increases the weight of the wine. Higher levels of residual sugar will do the same—just think of the rich, full-bodied "mouth feel" of a Port or other dessert wine. Keep in mind that alcohol derives from sugar; alcohol itself has a sweetness that plays a part in our assessment of a wine.

Another indicator of alcohol can be an actual sensation of heat in the mouth. This is usually raw and unpleasant and indicates an alcohol level too high for the other elements of the wine. But don't confuse heat with dryness or astringency. When your mouth and gums feel dry and "puckered up," you're reacting to the tannins in a wine, a substance derived from grape skins, seeds and stems, as well as from any wood the wine has been either fermented or aged in. Tannin gives structure to a wine and is a major factor in a wine's ability to age. But in a young or poorly made wine, you might think you've been chewing on a green two-by-four rather than drinking a glass of wine.

You'll notice that we've made no direct assessment of bitterness, as would be done in evaluating beer. Any excess bitterness in a wine is considered a negative characteristic and usually derives from crushed grape seeds, or pips, and the inclusion of green stems during fermentation. While bitterness is thus related to tannin levels, it signals sloppiness in the winemaking process. A bit of it can be pleasing; too much is quite unpleasant.

In beer, by contrast, bitterness is a welcome, even exciting flavor element, contributed by hops. It is this delicious bitterness that makes beer so refreshing and reflects its distinct style and the variety of hops used, as well as being the major player in balancing out the sweetness of the malt.

In fact (as you beer drinkers already know, but let it be mentioned in case a wine lover or two happens to be perusing), bitterness, as measured in IBUs, or international bitterness units, is one of the major measurements taken of any beer. And this scale can go to 100+. It's actually a calculation of the parts per million in the finished beer of the bitter iso-alpha acids derived from the hops and therefore not an ingredient found in wine. All very scientific.

A Bavarian weizen might come in at 12 or 14 IBU, a British pale ale at 30 to 50, an American craft IPA at 70 or 80 IBU.

THE PROCESS: PART 4—SWALLOW

As you swallow, focus on the flavors and the physical sensation of the wine. Too much alcohol at this point will definitely burn going down, and depending on the level of tannin, you'll experience either a smooth or rough lingering sensation when you swallow. One or two flavors are likely to dominate and stay with you for some period of time, maybe a couple of seconds, maybe a number of minutes. This is called the finish. And generally speaking, the longer the finish, the better the wine.

You'll note that there were major elements to the wine: acidity, sweetness, alcohol and tannins. When these blend harmoniously, a wine is said to be well balanced. No one element should dominate, nor should any be lacking. Too much acidity, relative to the other elements, makes a wine tart and green. Too little and it's flat and boring to taste. If a wine is low in acid and has soft tannins, it doesn't need a high alcohol level to please the palate. In fact, a high level of alcohol in such a wine would come across as hot and unpleasant.

On the other hand, a high level of sweetness, or alcohol, can offset the effects of a very tannic wine by blocking the sensation of astringency on the palate. We expect big red wines, especially when they're young, to have excess tannins, but these wines aren't really ready to drink yet. Once they age, the tannins will soften, the mouth feel will become much smoother and the wine will come into balance.

■ TECHNICAL DRIVEL ■

Now that you have the basics down, it's going to take some practice. (You hear that, Johnny? It's time for your homework. Go to your room and taste some wine, and don't come out until you're done!) The more you taste while paying attention to what you taste, the quicker you'll be able to recognize and assess a variety of wines. Don't rush. It takes time to learn to think about what you're drinking. And it helps if you can discuss your impressions—or lack of them—with someone else. So get to work, hopheads. It's time to pull the cork on another bottle and start sampling— responsibly, of course!

Oh, and one last thing. Wine writers like to be cute. No doubt you will hear such stimulating bromides as the "Five S's" or even the slightly more impressive "Six S's" when encountering certain educators or writers spewing forth on the techniques of tasting. Because "observe," "manipulate," "inhale," "taste," "swallow" and "reflect" do not, as a string of syllables, fall trippingly from the tongue, all wrapped in lovely alliteration, the wine world's august wordsmiths have taken it upon themselves to devise the "S's" concept. You'll note that in my judgment, beer drinkers, being of quick mind and impatient with foofaraw, would appreciate the abbreviated four S's used above. But just for your edification, should some ne'er-do-well toss this multi-S's malarkey at you in a social setting, challenging you to prove your wine worthiness, the S's are thus: "see," "swirl," "sniff," "sip," "swallow" and "savor," with it being permissible to substitute "sight" and "smell" where appropriate.

■ ■ ■ ■

The Good, The Bad & Keeping Score:
Remembering What You Like, & Why

Well, that was fun, all that drinking and thinking and note-taking. You *were* taking notes, weren't you? You should, because that's one of the best ways to learn and remember. Writing down your observations forces you to really think about the wine, to focus on what makes a wine exceptional, pretty good, or something you probably don't ever want to serve or drink again. It's surprising how quickly we lose track of the wines we've tasted—what was that gorgeous red we had last week with dinner, or that very elegant and complex French number that we tried at the local wine bar? Can you remember the name of that delicious white we had with those grilled prawns, or where it was from?

Every semi-serious grape nut takes notes, and most score the wines they taste. As you become more adept at this aspect of enjoying wine, you'll adopt your own shorthand. But for now, a little time spent recording your impressions will pay off in much greater knowledge and understanding of what you're drinking. Taking notes crystallizes your response to a particular wine as well as serving as your memory. Its importance can't be overstated if you sincerely wish to develop your wine smarts.

We'll get to the scoring aspect in a bit, but right now let's look at a simple tasting sheet that will serve our purposes quite well.

TASTING NOTES **Date:** _____ **Event:** _____

Wine _____ Vintage _____

Producer _____ Region _____

Varietal/blend _____ Price _____

(2) ___ Appearance: clarity, color, intensity _____
_____

(6) ___ Aroma/bouquet: forward, restrained, varietal_____
_____

(5) ___ Flavors: complex, simple, fruity, flawed _____
_____

(2) ___ Balance: acid, tannins, sugar/alcohol _____
_____

(1) ___ Body/texture: full, med, light; soft, chewy, hollow _____
_____

(2) ___ Finish/length: silky, smooth, harsh; extended, long, short_____
_____

(2) ___ Overall: _____
_____

(20) ___ Total score. Comments: _____
    <14 faulty; 14 below average; 15 average; 16 very good;
    17 excellent; 18 superior; 19-20 classic

This format keeps an accurate record of the wines you taste. There are many ways to score wine; here we use a 20-point system, and below is the more common 100-point system of wine critic Robert Parker. Based on grades given in school, many believe this system is more easily understood than the traditional 20-point approach. But so the beer drinkers of the world can move with ease through any gathering of wine geeks, we'll discuss them both!

Notice the 100-point system begins at 50. (Who said any of this was logical?) The wine gets 50 points just for showing up!

TASTING NOTES   *Date:* _____ *Event:* _____

Wine _____ Vintage _____

Producer _____ Region _____

Varietal/blend _____ Price _____

(5) ___ Appearance: clarity, color, intensity _____

___   _____

(10) ___ Aroma/bouquet: forward, restrained, varietal _____

_____

(15) ___ Flavors: complex, simple, fruity, flawed, balanced _____

_____

(10) ___ Finish/length: silky, smooth, harsh; extended, long, short

_____

(10) ___ Overall/aging potential: _____   _____

_____

(50) ___ plus 50 = _____ Total score

50-59 poor, unacceptable; 60-69 below average;
70-79 drinkable, with minor flaws;
80-89 above average to very good;
90-95 outstanding, exceptional; 96-100 classic, a great wine

Interesting, isn't it, how the twenty-point system actually records more diverse information than does the market-dominant 100-point system? But remember, the real value is to force you to focus on what's in your mouth, to move beyond "tastes like wine" and recognize the specifics of a wine's characteristics. It may be outstanding or flawed or good, but just not to your taste. With a little practice—that's right, you'll have to drink more—you will know *why* it's a good, great or poorly made wine.

So let's sip our way through an imaginary wine and score both these sheets. Actually, why not pour yourself a glass of something you've been wanting to try and assess it with me? Go ahead. I'll wait. In fact, I could use a glass myself. Let's see … red or white?

Ready? Great, so am I. And I chose a Shiraz, Australian, 2007, from the Barossa Valley, one of that country's best Shiraz regions. About two inches gets poured into a standard wine glass.

Recognize that wine lovers are a generous lot, a hopeful, optimistic breed with fingers crossed that a stellar experience will emerge from their glasses. So wine scoring is based on debits, take-aways from a perfect score rather than building a score from the ground up. In other words, we start at 20, or 100, and deduct points for less-than-perfect performance. We don't begin at zero and accumulate points for each positive quality of a wine. In any case, numerical score is just a bare-bones snapshot; it's the notes that carry the memory and remind us of a wine's particulars, of why we did or didn't enjoy it and whether it's a wine we should seek out or pass up in the future.

SIGHT:

At first glance the wine is very dark, almost a purple/black. Tilted at a 45-degree angle over a white tablecloth, it's apparent that the wine is clean and shiny and that its color runs right to the rim, also called the meniscus. (That's a good sign in that 2007 was a difficult year, with an early frost and late rain, two events that may dilute a wine and leave a telltale clear or watery meniscus.)

- **20-point system** – Nothing to debit here. Notes might read "dark purple/black hue, color to rim," 2 out of 2 points.

- **100-point system** – The same. Full 5 points awarded.

SWIRL:

First a quick sniff, then a good swirl, coating the inside of the glass. This wine is dark, even in a thin layer. The legs start slowly and slide down with medium viscosity and thickness. I would guess moderate to moderately high alcohol, 13.5% to 14.5%. A series of nose-in-the-glass inhalations offers aromas reminiscent of blackberry (to me), blueberry, maybe a bit of cinnamon and something I can't quite put my finger on. I try again, and again, without luck. Something's there, but what the heck is it? A few more tries and— voila— mint! Reminds me of chewing gum.

- **20-point system** – A bit disappointing. In an Aussie Shiraz it's nice to get a big nose, in-your-face aromas of dark berries, black pepper and spiciness. This wasn't bad, but I'll give it only 4½ out of 6 possible points for aroma.

- **100-point system** – 7 out of 10 points for aroma, with notes reading "quiet nose showing hints of blackberry and blueberry, cinnamon, a touch of mint."

SIP:

Take a medium-sized mouthful, enough to chew and swirl and gargle and coat your tongue and the insides of your mouth but not so much that you can't swallow or open your mouth to draw in some air. It's apparent there's a lot of fruit here. The wine is quite juicy—blackberry compote—and on further "chewing" of the wine, what seems to be dark plums. Nice, but not much else. It's also flabby, a term that connotes a lack of acid. Nor is there much in the way of tannin, the compound that makes your mouth and tongue, and even your gums pucker up. This wine is more akin to melted jam than a well-made, well-structured wine.

- **20-point system** – First, flavors. The wine was simple, with one dominant flavor, lacking in complexity, less than hoped for. 4 out of 5 points. Next, balance. As noted, the lack of acidity and noticeable tannins was a debit. I give it 1 out of 2 points. And finally, body. The weight of the wine was fine. It had no hollow points, and though it was jammy due to lack of acid, it wasn't either overly heavy (think a mouthful of cream) or light (like skim milk). So it gets 1 for 1 in this category.

- **100-point system** – Here, balance, texture and flavor are combined into a single 15-point category. The notes might read "a big mouthful of blackberry jam with a touch of dark plum, lacks complexity, no acid or tannins—simple and boring," 10 points.

SWALLOW:

Pay attention to the wine as it settles in your mouth and the physical sensation, in terms of intensity, texture and length of time the feeling lasts after you either spit the wine out (if you're tasting a number of wines) or swallow it.

After swallowing I'm left with a suggestion of tannins, but it's too little too late. The finish is only medium-long; ten or fifteen seconds after swallowing the wine has disappeared, leaving no lingering impression. A long, focused finish is the sign of a good wine; unfortunately, this one's not long enough to garner top marks.

- **20-point system** – Though the finish wasn't harsh, it certainly wasn't silky, nor was it long. We did, however, finally get the benefit of some tannin. 1½ points out of 2 in the finish category. As to the final "overall" impression, I'd debit the wine for a less-than-effusive nose, a simple flavor profile, lack of acidity and tannin and a merely average finish. 1 point out of 2.

- **100-point system** – A very average finish, in terms of both texture and length, earns 6 of a possible 10 points, while the overall impression does likewise, 6 of 10 points.

FINAL RESULTS:

Remember, the notes tell the tale. The numerical score is little more than a brief indicator of how much you like a particular wine on a particular day. It's entirely possible to try the same wine on different days under different circumstances and have a significant variation in scores.

How wine is bottled, transported, stored and prepared for tasting can all have an effect on how well it shows. You may notice in reading wine reviews that when a score seems abnormally high or low for a specific wine, based on its age and/or reputation, the review may include a footnote saying "tasted on multiple occasions with similar results" just to let you know the reviewer also questioned the initial score and wanted to be sure the wine was really as good or bad as indicated.

In the end, rating wines you taste will serve you well, providing a deeper appreciation of what you're drinking and of what you might wish to drink or buy in the future. Your wine-thinking and sensitivity to a wine's attributes will be more finely honed. It also helps you understand that a wine may score highly, be well made and without fault and still not be the type of wine you enjoy. Don't forget, there's a reason that wine professionals take notes.

Here's our 20-point scoring sheet after the tasting (the 100-point sheet would have similar notes and a total score of 84–34 from our assessment added to the base score of 50):

TASTING NOTES   *Date:* _____   *Event:* ___home tasting___

Wine ___XYZ Big Block Shiraz___ Vintage ____2007____

Producer ___Krazy Kangaroo Winery___ Region ___Barossa Valley___

Varietal/blend ____Shiraz____   Price ____$18____

(2) _2_ Appearance: clarity, color, intensity _very dark, purple/black_

___color goes to the rim___

(6) _4½_ Aroma/bouquet: forward, restrained, varietal _quiet, hints of_

___blackberry, blueberry, with a touch of pepper and mint___

(5) _4_ Flavors: complex, simple, fruity, flawed ___simple, blackberry,___

___with notes of licorice, although a touch jammy___

(2) _1_ Balance: acid, tannins, sugar/alcohol ___on the flabby side,___

___lacks tannin or structure___

(1) _1_ Body/texture: full, med, light; soft, chewy, hollow ___medium-___

___bodied, average weight___

(2) _1½_ Finish/length: silky, smooth, harsh; extended, long, short_____

___fairly smooth but not very long___

(2) _1½_ Overall: ___pleasing but no wow factor, average Aussie shiraz,___

___a bit flabby, not much complexity___

(20) _15½_ Total score. Comments: ___easy to drink, good everyday wine___

<14 faulty; 14 below average; 15 average; 16 very good;
17 excellent; 18 superior; 19-20 classic

■ ■ ■

6

Let The Liquid Be Your Guide: What Tasting Can Tell You

Before trying to impress your friends, however, let's go back to where we started. You now know *what* to look for in a wine—i.e., which observations are the relevant ones. So now that you've gathered the information that's important, the next step in the process is analyzing that information.

INTERPRETING THE INFO: PART 1—SIGHT

The tasting process began with sight, a visual assessment of the wine. A wine, especially a young wine, should be clean and clear, with good color and a bright reflective surface. Over a white background, look first straight down into a wine, then through it from the side, and finally assume the now-familiar 45-degree tilt to get a complete look at all of a wine's visual clues.

A cloudy or hazy appearance raises a red flag. You may have a wine that's unfiltered because the winemaker feels that filtering diminishes the wine's flavor or body. While it's not yet possible to make a definitive judgment, one generally likes to see a clean, clear wine in the glass. Haze in a wine can be serious; it may be a sign of yeast spoilage or a so-called protein haze (related to the bacterial haze sometimes seen in an older beer not pristinely made), but in either case it will negatively affect the wine's taste and is considered a defect. This is unlike a chill haze in beer, which is simply the harmless result of serving it too cold, though it does subdue the flavor somewhat.

What About Those Lazy, "Hazy" Days of Summer?
It's true that a chill haze in beer is unwelcome but not fatal. When thrown by an old lager, haze means it's time for a discard, and haziness in wine is almost always a bad sign. But let us not forget the scrumptious wheat beers, so perfect on those hot, summer days, and exemplified by the Hefeweizen. Hefe, which means "yeast" is meant to be enjoyed young, while Its cloudy, added dose of yeast is still contributing the richness and fruity flavors that are its hallmarks, and before it turns bad and spoils the brew.
The only real similarity in the world of wine is aging *sur lies*, or on the lees. When fermentation is complete, the spent yeast cells fall to the bottom of the fermentation tank and in most cases, the newly minted wine is pumped off to be bottled or aged in other vessels. In a few cases, though, such as good Chardonnays or Muscadets from France, the wine is allowed to remain on this creamy sludge of yeast cells, called lees, to enrich the body and texture of the wine and to add a distinctive flavor and creaminess. When bottled, however, the wine is racked off the lees, and the resulting juice is clear and able to live a long, tasty life.

Sediment or particles in a wine are usually harmless natural occurrences. In white wine, small grains that resemble salt crystals or tiny uniform bits of broken glass are most likely tartaric acid. Many wines undergo "cold stabilization" prior to bottling during which the temperature of a finished wine is lowered until the tartaric acid crystallizes and precipitates out as a harmless deposit. Still, it's not uncommon to find these tiny crystals in the bottom of a bottle or on the underside of the cork. Their presence may indicate a winemaker who prefers to fool around as little as possible with his or her wines, often a good thing.

In red wines, especially older vintages or wines made from deeply colored varietals, sediment forms as the color and tannin molecules bind together and drop out of solution. This is part of the normal course of aging and is the process responsible for the lightening of color and the increase in smoothness that comes from cellaring your best wines. This sediment, however, is gritty and not pleasant to drink—think coffee grounds in a fabulous cup of java. So either decant the wine before drinking or stand the bottle upright for a few hours so the sediment can fall to the bottom, and then pour carefully.

Bubbles and spritz should be present only in sparkling wines—i.e., Champagnes or wines labeled *sparkling, cremant, petilant, perlant* or *frizzante,* all meant to contain CO_2. You'll also find a few bubbles, intended to provide a refreshing quality, in Vinho Verde from Portugal, the occasional young white from Italy and in specific wines such as Lambrusco, a soft, fizzy red popular in its native Emilia region of Italy but without much presence in the U.S.

If, however, a non-sparkling wine shows a lot of bubbles, there is almost certainly a serious problem. A few random bubbles around the rim when a wine is first poured means nothing. But if the bubbles in a still (hence the term) table wine are numerous and persistent, it usually indicates a secondary fermentation occurring in the wine. This is not a good thing and means the original fermentation wasn't properly completed and the wine should never have been bottled. It's very likely the flavors will be off, funky, and unpleasant at best—you know, like skunked beer.

The color is both easy and complex. White wines range from almost clear to pale yellow with greenish glints to straw yellow to yellow to yellow gold to amber and even to golden brown. These terms are not absolute, but they should help you visualize the progression of possible colors. If you think a wine is buttercup yellow or brassy gold, record it as buttercup yellow or brassy gold.

On the red side, you might see anything from deep purple/ red with blue tints to dark ruby to brick red to garnet with amber highlights. In either case, white or red, the colors have been listed as they might appear going from youngest to oldest. In fact, color is one of a wine taster's best indicators. With age, whites tend to get darker and reds tend to lighten. So when tilting your glass at a 45-degree angle to visually inspect the wine, one of the main things to look for is the difference between the color in the center of the glass and at the rim. A red wine rim that's starting to look amber while the main color is a brick red is definitely older than a wine that's uniformly deep purple from center to edge.

You should also keep in mind that maturing wine in wood, which usually means oak barrels, accelerates the appearance of aging. Pour two young Chardonnays from the same vintage and region side by side. If one shows a deep yellow color and the other is quite pale in comparison, you can almost be sure the first was aged in oak, while the second spent its entire life in stainless steel tanks, and then into the bottle.

Most wines are made to be enjoyed within a year or two of their release. Nonetheless, the ability to age gracefully is considered a positive attribute. Should you pour a glass of young wine and find that its color is leaning to a dull, brownish mustard, it's a pretty good bet you have a wine that's gone bad. Brown or brown tinged color in a younger white usually means the wine is oxidized, probably the result of a poorly fitting cork that allowed a tiny stream of air to enter the bottle, inadequate sulfur additions during the winemaking process to protect the juice, or poor storage conditions before bottling. Another culprit could be improper storage after the wine was released. If your best friend has kept this bottle on a little countertop rack next to the stove for a year and a half, the wine has been "cooked," with the same end result. It's brown; it's bad.

Of course, this happens to red wines as well as white. It's just easier to spot these problems visually with whites, where the color shift is so obvious. With reds, you will learn to also depend on your nose and, to a lesser degree, your palate to root out these defects.

In general, a thick-skinned variety like Syrah or Shiraz, Cabernet Sauvignon or Zinfandel will be very dark when young; Tempranillo, Merlot and Sangiovese somewhat less so; and Grenache and Pinot Noir lighter still. Just as you would never confuse a stout with an amber ale, on sight alone a wine drinker would never confuse a Pinot Noir with a Cabernet Sauvignon, unless of course there was a wacky winemaker involved who thought everything should look and taste like a big Cabernet. Fortunately, that's a small and fast-dying breed.

Those gorgeous legs are an indicator of a wine's overall body. (That's wine-speak gone wrong!) As previously discussed, after a quick initial sniff, the wine should be swirled, coating the inside of the glass and thereby exposing a greater surface area to evaporation so its aromas can be more accurately assessed. Before planting your honker in the glass, however, take a gander at what's happening with the film of wine clinging to the inside of the glass.

Should the wine form a thin sheet of liquid that quickly runs back down the surface of the glass, the wine is probably light in body and low in alcohol and may even be from a cooler climate or a poor vintage. But if it hangs in place and only reluctantly breaks into a series of slowly descending tears, or legs, chances are the wine is higher in alcohol, fuller in body (it could even be sweet), and may be the product of a warmer climate or more favorable growing season.

INTERPRETING THE INFO: PART 2—SMELL

Moving from sight to smell, the next job is to analyze the information provided by a wine's aromas and/or its bouquet. Much of the pleasure, as well as the sensual information about a wine, is found in the nose.

A good wine smells and tastes "as it should" for the type of grapes from which it's made. For the most part, good Cabernet Sauvignons exhibit a strong similarity to one another as far as aromas and flavors are concerned. As do Merlots or Syrahs or Sauvignon Blancs or Rieslings. Naturally there are variations depending on locale, climate, soil (all part of what is known as *terroir*), winemaking, aging and other factors. Even so, a good Syrah smells and tastes like Syrah, and with some experience you should be able to identify it as such.

When a wine smells and tastes like it should for the type of grape or grapes from which it's made, the wine is referred to as "varietally correct," a desirable quality. We like a wine to be what it's supposed to be. So when assessing a wine's aroma, we want it to be typical of its varietal. In cases where the aroma is well defined but not specific to a grape type or types, we refer to it as merely "distinctive." This could be the case where a wine has a nose of boysenberry and vanilla but doesn't tell us any more. It may be a pleasing wine to drink, but it's not likely to be a great wine.

Aroma provides information about important elements in a wine's makeup. First, the fruit smells tell us about the grape variety, as discussed above. Second, the earthy smells, of minerals, rocks and dirt, and even local vegetation, tell us still more about the *terroir*, that fancy French term that encompasses all aspects of place: soil type, elevation, drainage, weather, orientation to the sun, length of growing season, etc. And third, the winemaking itself is responsible for a whole slew of aromas that also give clues as to the wine's type and origin. These include aromas of oak, cedar, leather, tobacco, coffee, chocolate, vanilla, smoke, coconut, and toast.

And once you're a bit more experienced with older wines, you'll recognize a fourth facet of aroma: a wine's bouquet.

> **Aren't Bouquet and Aroma the Same Thing?**
> Well, not really. It's true the terms are often used interchangeably, but bouquet is a specific set of aromatic impressions that result from bottle age. Young wines don't have a bouquet; though they may be beautifully aromatic, showing a nose of many splendors; bouquet is not among them.
> A wine that has aged, that has reached the point where its bright, individual fruit aromas are softening into a delicious mixed-fruit pie, as focused on the crust as on the filling, where the oak-imparted aromas of vanilla or coconut are gaining a nutty complexity, where the tannins have softened, and those matured and mellowed volatiles have lost their edge and exist in harmony with one another, where even a hint of oxidation, of the wine's ultimate demise, is woven softly into the background, is a wine that exhibits bouquet.

Does this wine stink? Hopefully not. At least not beyond the earthy, gamey aromas typical of syrah or good merlot, not beyond the "barnyard" nose of a beautiful Burgundy. But if you smell freshly struck matches, boiled cabbage, vinegar, nail-polish remover, wet dog, wet cardboard, or any other foul, swampy odor, you probably have a glass of faulty wine.

The smell of matches or cabbage comes from an excess of sulfur in the wine. Try decanting the wine for a short period of time. The sulfur might dissipate; if not, at this point there's no cure. Sulfur has been used in winemaking since ancient times as a preservative to retard bacterial growth and prevent oxidation of the grape juice, just as you might squeeze lemon juice over freshly cut apples to keep them from browning. In some wineries it's also used to prepare barrels for aging the wine, again to prevent spoilage. Unfortunately, there are winemakers with too heavy a hand when it comes to the addition of sulfur, but most winemakers prefer using as little as possible and the industry is working hard to reduce the need for additional sulfur.

■ TECHNICAL DRIVEL ■

There are people who claim susceptibility to sulfur headaches and posit a number of particulars in support of their assertion. One that's commonly heard is that red wine causes them great distress, though drinking white wine isn't a problem. Interestingly, more sulfur is used to protect white wines, which lack the phenolic protection (derived from the color compounds and tannins in the grape skins used in red wine fermentation). Sulfur is also used as a preservative in many fruit juices and in most dried fruit. So if a person has no problem eating dried fruit or drinking white wine, it's a good bet their headache comes from some other source.

The smell of vinegar or nail-polish remover is an indication that bacteria are beginning the unwelcome chemical conversion of alcohol into vinegar, possibly due to less than stringent conditions in the winery and/or an imbalance between alcohol (too much) and acid levels (too little) in a warmer wine region. If the process is just beginning and the smell not too off-putting, drink the wine and enjoy. If the smell or taste is clearly unpleasant, the wine is spoiled.

Wet or moldy cardboard is the signature smell of a "corked" wine—i.e., one suffering from 2,4,6-trichloroanisole contamination, or TCA. This bane of the wine world results from an undetectable fungus growing within perfectly healthy, normal-looking cork. It happens, and it ruins as much as 5% to 8% of all wines sealed with cork. This nasty little compound can even take root in the wooden barrels, pallets and structural elements in a winery, causing a major and very expensive headache that can ruin the facility's entire output.

Other off-odors result from improper cleaning of filter pads or the growth of particular bacteria in and around fermentation equipment. Wine is a food; it should be clean and fresh and smell healthy and inviting. If you run across an obviously faulty bottle of wine, stick the cork back in and return it to your retailer. No honest or reputable wine dealer would ever refuse to refund a bad bottle, except in states where it's actually illegal to do so.

Clues to what's in the glass are found in a grape variety's signature wine aromas. For example, a scent of dark berries and green pepper with notes of pencil lead and tobacco would point to Cabernet Sauvignon, while red fruits like strawberry and rhubarb with hints of black tea are typical descriptors for Pinot Noir. But it's more than just memorizing a matrix of aromas. It's first of all about focusing your sniffer and letting the scents and volatile compounds waft up to the receptor site in your retro-nasal cavity. Then relax, and let your brain run through all the possible associations you might personally have with a given set of aroma compounds.

In time you will begin to make the associations of aroma and varietal. At first, whether you smell cherry and I smell raspberries isn't really the issue. The concept is that a certain set of aromas is common to wine from certain grape varieties. So one taster may claim to be delighted with the black cherry, green olive, and cooked meat aromas of a favorite Sangiovese while another equally practiced palate may identify exactly the same wine from the red cherry, orange peel and earthy characteristics that he or she perceives. Yet to both, the wine is clearly a specific varietal. So when tasting, write down whatever fruit or other odors *you* discover in the glass.

Some aromas are more clearly delineated. Vanilla is usually vanilla, and coconut is hard to call anything else, and both mean aging, probably in new oak. Green pepper is another food smell that's pretty clear-cut, though depending on its pungency some may call it simply vegetal and in other cases it can even be identified as smelling like cat's pee. Mmmmm. But in all cases, it indicates a wine from a cool growing region and/or grapes that were picked before they were fully mature.

Spicy, as in black or white pepper, cloves, mint, anise, etc., may reflect the varietals Syrah, Nebbiolo, Pinotage, or may be the residual effect of a strain of yeast or a result of barrel maturation. Citrus aromas indicate good acid levels in a wine and can be found in both red and more commonly white wines. Berry fruits—blackberry, raspberry, black raspberry, strawberry, currants, boysenberry, mulberry—are most common to red wines, being derived from the chemical compounds found in the red grape skins and pulp. Tropical fruits tend more to white wines, with their gorgeous lychee, kiwi and pineapple notes, though many whites feature apple and pear as well.

If a wine is positively stony, minerally, and without the richness of fruit you had expected, you're experiencing *terroir*, the flavor of the soil coming through, as might be the case with a Chablis, a crisp and structured Chardonnay from the north end of Burgundy. In many wines from the South of France, you'll detect wild herbs and hints of rosemary and thyme, a telling reminder of the *garrigue*, the wild, low-lying plants that carpet windy hillsides above the Mediterranean. A warm snootful of rich cooked fruits, of dates and figs in your glass, will tell you something else; it may point to a warm climate, southern Italy perhaps, and the Negroamaro grape, or it may be the sign of a wine that is aging rapidly, too rapidly, perhaps a product of the devastatingly hot 2003 vintage across much of Europe.

You'll get few definitive answers from this step alone. In assessing a wine, it's the cumulative evidence that tells the tale. Sight will provide initial clues; smell will expand on them. And they may not agree with each other. However, nosing a wine, whether for aroma or bouquet, for hints to a wine's identity in a blind tasting or for the simple pleasure of enjoying it before taking a sip, is a direct path to understanding and appreciation.

INTERPRETING THE INFO: PART 3—SIP

A good sip, swished in the mouth, coating the tongue and palate and all the soft tissues, slurped and worked to mix with oxygen, held for a bit to let the wine work its magic, is the premier event in wine tasting. Yes, smell is crucial—the nose reveals volumes—but with the mouth in play, too, it's possible to add the sweet, sour, bitter, salty and umami components that underpin the subtleties of aroma. It's also in the mouth that we get the true sense of weight and texture that are likewise so much a part of the wine-appreciation experience.

There is actually more involved with the sip than with the smell. When nosing a wine to capture the clues of aroma, one need concentrate only on the smell, the aroma, the volatile compounds entering the nasal cavity—whatever you choose to call it. A singular event. Sniff, then pay attention.

But when tasting the wine, you're participating in the most sensual, as in "engaging the senses," aspect of all.

- First, you're using the taste buds to pick up the five flavor elements and all the degrees and combinations thereof.

- Second, the tongue and soft palate are assessing the weight or fullness of the wine.

- Third, additional tactile sensations like dryness and heat are also being recognized and measured.

- Fourth, vapors—i.e., the volatile compounds (their release stimulated by the heat of your mouth)—are escaping out the back of your mouth and up your retro-nasal cavity to contact the same cluster of nerve endings used when sniffing.

So in a sense, when you "taste," you're just adding new steps while you continue to smell. (Well, *you* don't smell … hopefully, but you get the point.) With a mouthful of wine, well slurped and sending messages to tongue, taste buds, gums, hard and soft palates, and even up your nose, albeit from the inside, there's a lot of info to judge and juggle.

Let's start with the taste buds. By now you realize that specific areas on your tongue don't pick up only specific tastes, as once was thought. It may be true, for example, that the tip of the tongue is most sensitive to sweetness, but it's not unaware of salty, bitter, sour or umami. And taste buds cover almost all areas inside the mouth, not just the tongue, so the overall sensations of the basic flavor elements come as well from the back of the throat, the roof of the mouth, etc. Another realization is that we all have differing thresholds for perceiving and identifying various taste elements. One person might think a wine shows some residual sugar, while another may detect no sweetness at all.

Sweet   That said, in a dry wine (one not intended to be a dessert or sweet wine) a hint of sweetness may indicate that a fermentation wasn't fully completed, leaving a small amount of fruit sugar unconverted to alcohol. Since sweetness gives wine a sensation of greater body and richness, this bit of residual sugar may have been intended by the winemaker. Zinfandels are often made in this style, and some styles of Riesling purposely retain sugar to balance their piercing acidity. Or it may be that in a wine like Cabernet Sauvignon, the yeast petered out before completing their job because the fermentation was allowed to run too hot, appropriate yeast nutrients weren't added to the mix, or some other shortcoming occurred in the winery. More than a suggestion of sweetness in a dry wine is not desirable.

Some fruit-forward styles of wine may *seem* to be sweet when in fact they are completely dry. The richness of the overall flavors combined with the perception of sweetness given off by high levels of alcohol can be tricky to distinguish from actual residual sugar.

Sour Wine tasters generally use the term *tart* rather than *sour* and measure this component by assessing a wine's acidity. Without acidity, a wine lacks zip and is referred to as flabby. Acidity livens food and makes it more appealing—hence squeezing lemon over fish to bring out the flavors—and a good food wine has enough acid to stimulate the palate in just the same way. Acidity in grapes is a natural component and gradually lessens as the grapes ripen. If picking is done too late or temperatures in a vineyard have been too high, the resulting wine will often lack acidity.

Most red and many white wines undergo a second fermentation called malolactic fermentation, to convert tart malic acid into softer lactic acid and to add complexity. So while too little acidity subtracts from a wine's ability to give pleasure and accompany food, too much makes it harsh and unpleasant to drink.

When you taste a wine that just lies in your mouth like old fruit juice—a flabby wine, in other words—there's a good chance the fruit was left too long before picking, perhaps in hopes that more "hang time" on the vine would increase its flavor. Unfortunately, it does little more than tire the palate. And when you come across a wine with too much acidity, a sour, tart wine, it's either an example of a very food-oriented, Old World wine style or simply not well made.

Salty About the only wine you're likely to taste with an actual hint of saltiness to it would be a Sherry from the Jerez region of Spain. Otherwise, salt isn't a common, or welcome, flavor in wine and is seldom encountered.

Bitter   Most wines have some bitterness, and in small amounts this isn't a problem. Reds may show bitterness in the finish, and many Italian whites are noted for flavors of bitter almond in the mouth. High levels of bitterness, though, can result from too many stalks and leaves being left in the fermenter, a sign of laziness on the winemaker's part.

Umami   Savory, meaty, slightly pungent flavors and sensations, though most obvious in foods like soy sauce and mushrooms, are far from uncommon in wine, red or white. Where wines are aged *sur lie,* they absorb amino acids and other compounds that contribute to the level of umami. So finding umami in a white wine may point directly to *sur lie* aging, intended to increase the weight and richness of what might otherwise be a rather innocuous light-bodied wine. In red wines, one is most apt to encounter umami in big, rich wines made from grapes with high ripeness levels or in older wines that have aged in the bottle, as a so-called "reductive" environment (where little or no oxygen is present) also encourages the development of umami.

While umami *in* beer often signals a brew left for too long on its yeast, beer does a remarkable job of pairing *with* umami-rich foods. Think of a juicy burger with cheese and grilled mushrooms or that MSG-delicious Chinese dish that's so hard to pair with wine.

This is where the properly chosen beer can shine. What better than a lusty brown ale or Irish stout to bring out the best in that beefy, cheesy, mushroom combo, or a crisp, hoppy lager with your favorite Oriental dish—unless it happens to be spicy hot, in which case something malty, maybe a Witbier or an Oktoberfest, would be the perfect match.

Weight   This refers to the viscosity of a wine, influenced by alcohol and sugar and phenolics, and is easily and immediately apparent when a liquid is put in the mouth. We've discussed the old standby for understanding weight when referring to wine—think of a light-bodied wine as having a mouth feel similar to skim milk, a medium-bodied wine more like 2% milk, and a full-bodied wine having the weight and richness of whole milk.

In general, dry white wines will be lighter-bodied than red wines. They often have a lower alcohol level, and they certainly have fewer of the heavy color molecules known as phenolics. Any wine with high alcohol, like a big red, or with lots of sugar, like most dessert wines, will feel heavier in the mouth.

Tannin   In concert with a variety of chemical compounds, tannin is the primary culprit behind the dryness, or astringency, of a wine and is derived from grape stems, seeds and skins and from the oak barrels in which wine is matured. It may be classed as fine-grained, well integrated, green, coarse, smooth, dusty, or harsh depending on the feel and texture and effect it has on the palate, gums and, at times, even the teeth. It's the pucker factor; the structure in a wine, the framework on which everything else—fruit and flavor, sugar and alcohol—is hung.

Big tannins are to be expected in many young red wines, especially those made from Cabernet Sauvignon, Syrah, Tannat, or Nebbiolo. As wines age, the tannins soften and become less obtrusive. Some wine drinkers like the bold, almost-brawny feel of these young reds and enjoy drinking newly released Bordeaux, Barolos and other highly tannic wines; others would rather wait a few years for the gentler, more subtle creature most of these wines will become.

Big powerful tannins always signal a young wine. If you're tasting blind, the intensity of the tannins can also be an indicator of varietal. No matter how it's made, Beaujolais, for example, a wine made from the Gamay grape, will never show much tannin, as it's a thin-skinned grape with little natural tannin to begin with.

Tannin is also a key component in wines that will age well, so any wine destined for the cellar should have a good level of tannins. What no taster wants to find are hard green tannins such as you might encounter when chewing seeds from unripe table grapes; this indicates a wine made of immature grapes or with too many stems included, probably having less fruitness than it should, and unlikely to age well. As a wine mellows with time, big tannins will soften, but harsh green tannins will always be harsh and green.

■ TECHNICAL DRIVEL ■

Astringency in wine is caused by numerous naturally occurring chemicals in addition to tannin, the main ones being polyphenols, which includes resveratrol and other related antioxidants that have gotten so much press in recent years, and flavonoids, including anthocyanins, the color molecules that make a red wine red and which are a natural component of grape skins. Since the juice used in making white wine is removed from its seeds and skins almost immediately to prevent the wine from picking up any color, most white wines have far less tannin than do reds.

Tannin molecules are large, one reason they're so noticeable in the mouth, and as wine ages, the tannin molecules bind with anthocyanins, forming long, heavy chains that fall to the bottom of the bottle as sediment. It's this action that causes wine to soften as it ages and is responsible for the color shift from dark to lighter red that's characteristic of an older wine.

Alcohol Formed as the result of fermentation, wherein yeast convert sugar into ethyl alcohol and carbon dioxide—the reason for the fermentation in the first place. Otherwise we'd all be drinking plain old grape juice! Wine is about 85% water, 14% alcohol and 1% other flavonoids and phenols. When the alcohol level is too high, it is perceived on the palate as both hot and sweet and leaves a burning sensation in the back of the throat. This may occur because the grapes were picked late, with a high level of sugar resulting in a high level of alcohol, possibly due to style (as in red Zinfandel), an exceptionally hot year or climate (2003 across Europe or most any vintage in Australia) and/or less-than-stellar winemaking.

Balance   The key to a good wine and essential in a great one. An often confusing term, *balance* simply means that the acid, fruit, alcohol content, tannin, sugar and other sensory impressions of a wine are in harmony, according to the wine's type and style. No one element should overwhelm the others. If a wine is hot and leaves an unpleasant burn in your throat, it's out of balance. If the acidity is so low you're not sure whether you're drinking wine or melted jam or so high that you shudder when you swallow, it's likewise out of balance. If there's a distinct impression of sugar in a dry red wine, or a particular flavor in any wine, be it green pepper or citrus or coconut, that stands out so distinctly that it blocks any other, the wine is unbalanced. As to style, typicity, etc., a well-made white should have enough acidity to refresh the palate, while a young red can be excused a good dose of tannin if it's intended to age and reach its peak only after a number of years in the cellar.

INTERPRETING THE INFO: PART 4—SWALLOW

There are times when a flavor or characteristic becomes magnified after swallowing, but usually it's the textural aspect and the length of sensation that are the keys to a wine's finish. A smooth, even silky feel when swallowing indicates that a wine's tannins have lost their aggressive quality through age or good winemaking, while a rough or unbalanced sensation tells us we're drinking a young, unresolved wine—fine if it's a wine meant to be laid down but a definite fault in a wine intended for immediate consumption.

Length, the other aspect of finish, refers to the duration of a wine's aftertaste. Is all sensation gone within a few seconds of swallowing, or does the taste, the impact, the aroma of a wine linger in your mouth and on your palate for a more prolonged period? In general, a longer finish (in some wines the finish seems to go on and on after spitting or swallowing) indicates a higher-quality wine. Length is driven by the totality of fruit and polyphenols and acidity, so after swallowing, give your palate, and yourself, a chance to gauge and enjoy this marker of quality. Relax. Reflect. This stuff isn't for chugging, you know.

■ ■ ■ ■

Blah, Blah, Blah:
Decoding Snobby Wine Talk

Is anything worse than listening to a roomful of wine snobs dribble on about "the lovely bouquet" or a wine that's "rich and full-bodied yet racy and svelte"? It seems they speak a language only distantly related to our own. Sure, it's based on the same words we use, but in arrangements that can border on the ridiculous. And yet they go on for hours, tasting wine after wine and following each with a stream of babble that seems to make no sense.

The amazing thing is that they appear to understand each other and to get great pleasure from these seemingly inane conversations. If so, there might be some method to this verbal madness, and perhaps even something to be gained from understanding it.

The problem, and it's one we all have, is that most languages have a limited capacity to describe flavors and aromas. Think about this for a minute: we can describe buildings or people or attitudes or objects or a landscape we've seen in great detail, painting precise and vivid pictures that effectively communicate our thoughts, feelings and impressions. But try describing the taste of a blueberry.

Not so easy, is it? How about the smell of soap—not per-fumed, just plain old soap? Or the taste of a cucumber, the flavor of a carrot, the smell of a freshly cut tomato, or the aroma of a rose or a walk through the woods? Can you adequately describe any of these? Few people can, even though we can all identify these smells and flavors when we encounter them. We're just not taught how to discuss flavor or aroma, and our languages don't have the words to do so.

Which brings us back to the winos at the tasting. They're all fans of a beverage that has hundreds of subtle and not-so-subtle variations. They're also fans of a beverage that can be fairly costly and that is stunningly good when it's at its best. For all these rea-sons, it makes sense that wine lovers would want, would need, some way to communicate and share impressions about wine. Since we all have individual preferences, it isn't enough to simply say a wine tastes good or bad. According to whom? You may love a wine that I don't really care for, or vice versa. Do you want to spend money on a wine just because I say it's good, without knowing why?

Yes, it may be good. It may be a quite well-made wine, but also one that isn't to your taste. This means that a more detailed, descrip-tive and evaluative language, commonly understood, is necessary for one wine drinker to intelligently discuss wine with another.

Since no such descriptive aspect is part and parcel of modern language, wine enthusiasts (drinkers, growers, vintners, etc.) have developed their own lingo, and like all languages, it has evolved and matured over the years. It naturally borrows heavily from sensuous (i.e., of the senses) verbiage and is filled with references to all sorts of smells and flavors but also to sight, to touch and even to human emotion and characteristics.

Though instances and mentions of wine go back to ancient times, with such precise and insightful declarations as "a fine drink" and "pleasing in great measure," it was during the twen-tieth century that writing for the customer, as opposed to the trade, really came of age, spearheaded by the English. They were, to be sure, heavily influenced by the French, from whom they bought most of what they drank (and still do). Their wine language and descriptions borrowed heavily from sensuous, even sexual verbiage, and at times it was hard to tell if certain writers were describing wine or recording their own erotic daydreams.

Tasting notes in those days were replete with references to "voluptuousness" and "sex appeal" and other such phrasing that had little or nothing to do with the contents of a wine glass. More recently, at least since the 1980s, an outburst of American wine writing has retreated from the sensual and moved toward comparing wine to things we have probably smelled or tasted. Wine-speak can actually be very creative, helping expand the ability to understand, identify and describe the world.

And so, enough with the preliminaries. On to the specifics.

THE OBVIOUS:

Assorted fruit and vegetable aromas and flavors:

Apple	Dates	Mint
Apricot	Fig	Orange
Banana	Grapefruit	Peach
Bell pepper	Grass	Pear
Blackberry	Green olive	Pineapple
Black cherry	Kiwi	Plums
Black olive	Lemon	Prune
Blueberry	Lime	Raisin
Cassis	Lychee	Raspberry
Cherry	Melon	Strawberry

Whoa, whoa, whoa! What are you talking about?
There are no figs or green olives in *my* glass of wine.

■ TECHNICAL DRIVEL ■

Q: None of those items, with the exception of grapes, are actually in wine, are they? (Not unless the discussion has moved to fruit wines.) So why are they listed, and why are they part of wine-speak?

A: That's right, none of the fruits or vegetables listed above, excepting grapes, is found in the type of wine we're talking about. But the same or very similar chemical compounds do exist in wine as in a variety of other foods and organic substances.

For example, consider the phenolic compound $C_{10}H_{12}O_2$, also known as frambinone, oxyphenylon, or rasketone and commonly called raspberry ketone. As you may have guessed, it's the primary aroma element in raspberries and is also present in wine!

So while verbal jousting over whether a wine offers aromas of cherry or strawberry or of blackberry or blueberry may be pointless and very much a case of "in the nose of the beholder," there are real and definite chemical relationships between common tastes and aromas and those drifting up to our olfactory receptors from a glass of wine.

Now it gets easier to understand a taster who swirls and sniffs and samples a glass of Chardonnay and raises her head to say, "*This is bursting with green apple and pear and even has a touch of fig in the background.*" Basic wine-speak. Unadorned. She has simply absorbed the volatile compounds in the wine and related them to smells and aromas she already knows.

THE LESS OBVIOUS:

Flavors and aromas also present that derive from fermentation and aging, either in wood (usually oak) or in bottle. As wine is made and ages, the many compounds it's composed of interact with each other, with whatever oxygen the wine comes into contact with, and with natural compounds from oak barrels, creating entirely new chemical combinations and aromas.

Derived from fermentation and aging in oak:

- Almond
- Bread
- Butter
- Butterscotch
- Caramel
- Cedar
- Clove
- Coconut
- Creamy
- Graphite
- Nutty
- Spicy
- Smoky
- Toasty
- Vanilla
- Yeasty

Derived from bottle aging:

- Bacon
- Barnyard
- Chocolate
- Cigar box
- Coffee
- Earthy
- Gamey
- Honey
- Leather
- Soy sauce
- Tobacco
- Tar

And now the basis for tasting notes and wine-speak like "wonderful aromas of cassis and dark plums, with a backdrop of leather and tobacco, followed by a hint of chocolate on the finish."

So far, it's all pretty straightforward, or at least understandable. And while it might take a bit of practice (and confidence in your own perceptions) to spout forth, it's become apparent that there's no mystery here. However …

From here, things get a bit more dicey. Casual beer aficionados may content themselves with an assessment of a beer's color or the robustness of its flavor, while the cognoscenti get quite specific, appraising major characteristics such as color (SRM), bitterness (IBU) and gravity in precise, quantifiable terms. These are scientific measurements and have much to do with whether a beer is judged as good, great or should-have-stayed-at-home.

In comparison, wine assessment—or "sensory evaluation" if you'd like to adopt the high-falutin' term—is, at its extreme, downright imprecise. Official scorecards aside, wine drinkers runneth over with zip lingo and arcane language used to supplement the relatively straightforward fruit, fermentation and aging terms mentioned above.

Beer drinkers drink and then they talk. About the beer, and then about sports, politics, work, and, of course, the opposite sex. And wine drinkers drink and then *they* talk. About the wine, and then even more about the wine, and then about sports, politics, work, and the opposite sex. And often about the wine again, although by this time in language that many find indecipherable. And so, sports fans, on to advanced wine-speak.

THE BARELY OBVIOUS:

Subjective, interpretive, insider-oriented and in need of definitions:

- **Agreeable**—pleasing, with good fruit, well made, not too much of anything

- **Aggressive**—reasonably well balanced but with big, somewhat hard tannins and/or high alcohol or acidity

- **Austere**—with a good streak of tannin or acidity or both but lacking in fruit or alcohol "fatness"

- **Chunky**—medium- to full-bodied, decent tannin, shows more leather, tobacco, smoky notes

- **Closed**—lacking aroma, very little smell

- **Clumsy**—the product of poor winemaking, out of balance, too much alcohol or tannin, feels manipulated

- **Complex**—showing at least three or more distinct identifiable flavors

- **Dumb**—a wine that has aged beyond its youthful freshness and exuberance but hasn't yet developed the appealing aspects of maturity, often used in reference to Bordeaux of ± 5 to 8 years

- **Delicate**—light- to medium-bodied, low alcohol, noticeable if slight tannin

- **Earthy**—a positive when referring to characteristics of soil (chalky, minerally) but a negative when it refers to a moldy or cabbage aroma

- **Effusive**—great volatiles, extremely aromatic

- **Fat**—full-bodied with good alcohol

- **Faulty**—a flawed wine with serious chemical or bacteriological problems

- **Feminine**—light- to medium-bodied, often characterized by red fruit flavors such as strawberry and cherry, as opposed to heavier black fruits like blackberry and cassis; also has a freshness derived from a bit more acid and a bit less alcohol or tannin

- **Flabby**—unbalanced, specifically lacking in acidity, dull on the palate

- **Generous**—good fruit, pleasing alcohol, may or may not be complex but certainly enjoyable

- **Grip**—the textural feel of a wine on the palate

- **Hollow**—lack of sensation or weight when held in the mouth

- **Insipid**—drinkable but boring, without pleasure, often reflective of the low-quality end of mass-produced wine

- **Integrated**—a wine in which disparate elements have come together as desired during aging

- **Long**—an extended finish, a wine with flavors and mouth feel that continue well after swallowing

- **Masculine**—full-bodied, displaying big tannin, high alcohol and dark fruit, leather and spiciness

- **Mouth feel**—the overall sensation of weight, texture, flavors, alcohol, etc., of a wine on the tongue and palate

- **Persistent**—lingering sensation, not fading away

- **Quaffable**—easy to drink, not necessarily great but enjoyable

- **Reticent**—closed, not open with either aromas or flavor

- **Rich**—well-developed fruit flavors, may indicate ripe fruit or a small amount of residual sugar or both

- **Rustic**—an indigenous wine made in the local, traditional manner, may seem a bit rough or unharmonious

- **Silky**—an extremely smooth finish, perfectly integrated tannins, not too much alcohol or acidity, nothing harsh

- **Structure**—the backbone of a wine, refers to levels of tannin

And that's just a smattering. But if you can get a sense of these terms and their connections and references to wine, you'll be well on your way to understanding the most obtuse wine-speak.

The wine was deep-hued, dark ruby-violet running clear to the edge. It opened with effusive aromas of rich blackberry, cassis, a hint of smoke and a slight gaminess. On the palate it was big and fat, overblown with blackberry, blueberry, white pepper and cooked bacon. Full-bodied, great mouth feel, with a persistent, focused finish.

By now, that kind of description should make perfect sense. So try this one:

An oil-drilling roughneck of a wine, fills your head with a gusher of big black aromas. This wine is all muscle and sinew, and when it grabs hold, it won't let go. Not for the fainthearted.

Or these:

At first as shy as a blushing schoolgirl, until rosy cheeks betray the come-hither glance of dark, piercing eyes, leading to a voluptuous display of rich, ripe fruit and a sprinkling of cinnamon and spice, lively and caressing on the tongue. A lovely wine to brighten a rainy afternoon before the fireplace.

An insouciant little number, a bit racy yet with a reassuring firmness. Tart but not sour, flashy enough to keep one's interest through a plate of oysters, horseradish and more.

Now that's wacky wine talk, the last two of a style seldom seen these days. Even so, after gaining familiarity with various levels of wine-speak, it's mostly understandable. So wine geekdom or not, if you have a basic foundation in the vocabulary of wine, even the silly, snobby chitchat makes sense.

■　■　■　■

8

Major Grapes & Secret Aliases: What's in the Bottle & What To Expect

D o you remember the first time you bought a beer you'd never tried before, or even heard of? Maybe it was a bock, or a bitter, or a Belgian dubbel or a barley wine. It might have been an IPA or an ESB or perhaps an Irish amber or a Dortmunder export. And you may have been delighted with your purchase, discovering a beverage that was new, different and delicious. Or maybe not. If you were expecting a clean, clear swallow of pilsner-like purity and instead got a smoky, meaty mouthful of märzen rauchbier, you may have wondered how a beer could taste like a ham sandwich toasted over a burning tire and why such a thing should even exist.

Had someone given you a heads-up and provided you with advance info as to what those beers were all about, it might have led to a better tasting experience or at least kept you from slowing down your experimentation when nothing seemed to be what you had expected. So it follows that a brief look at grape types and wine styles should assist the novice guzzler in choosing the wines he or she is most interested in trying and most likely to enjoy.

It should also prevent confusion about what's actually in the many types of wine that don't name the grape or grapes used to produce them. Most of these are Old World wines (European) that have long been named for their place of origin or production. New World wines, on the other hand (practically everything other than European), are typically labeled varietally, so as a consumer you have a head start on judging what's being poured into your glass.

Because while the manner and location of growing wine grapes—how densely together the vines are planted, how severely they're pruned, how much water they're given, what kind of soil they're planted in, etc. (collectively known as viticulture)—and the way in which they're fermented and aged—in an open or closed container, with natural or introduced yeast, at high temperature or low, aged in oak barrels or stainless steel (collectively known as viniculture)—have a major impact on the way a wine tastes, the biggest determinant of wine flavor is the variety of grape from which it's made.

While on the subject of New World vs. Old, it's helpful to understand that New World wines tend to be more fruit-driven, often with higher alcohol levels, while Old World examples strive for a more restrained commingling of multiple elements, including the fruit but also incorporating minerality, balance, *terroir*, etc. Neither style is right or wrong, though many people do prefer one over the other. And New or Old World labels aside, there are winemakers in Australia or America who favor an Old World approach and winemakers in Europe who are just as committed to showcasing the wine's fruit.

Just as certain cultivars of hops are referred to as the noble hops—specifically Hallertau, Tettnanger, Spalt, and Saaz, each named for the region or city where they are primarily grown—and so designated as they're used more for their aromatic effects than as bittering agents in beer, so too does the wine world have its noble varietals.

In truth, this designation isn't much used anymore, for a variety of reasons, but it typically refers to grapes capable of producing not just good but great wines, and of being successfully grown in multiple regions and *terroirs*. Though many "authorities" insist on including Chenin Blanc, Sémillon and/or Syrah on the list, all will agree that Chardonnay, Riesling, Sauvignon Blanc, Cabernet Sauvignon, Merlot, and Pinot Noir comprise the six classic noble grapes.

THE MOST-LIKELY-TO-ENCOUNTER WHITE VARIETIES

1.) **Chardonnay**—easily grown, a worldwide favorite, relatively high alcohol, not overly aromatic; shows green apple, pear, grapefruit and notes of honey when sourced from a cool climate; mango, melon, peach and pineapple with a definite fullness when grown in warmer climes. The white grape mostly likely to be oak aged, which adds a layer of smokiness, butterscotch, and toast as well as deepening the hue to a lovely golden yellow.

2.) **Riesling**—prefers a cool climate, best examples from Germany, Austria, Alsace, Australia, Washington state. Dazzling acidity and crisp flavors are its hallmark. Seldom oaked, pale color, very aromatic, may smell of petrol and wet slate, can be sweet, off-dry or dry, with a quite minerally character. Peach, green apple, lime, grapefruit, and lychee are common descriptors.

3.) **Sauvignon Blanc**—has great personality, best from the Loire Valley of France, New Zealand, Italy, South Africa, Australia, Chile, and the U.S., medium-pale straw color, has a wonderful herbal freshness, high notes of cut grass, green pepper and kiwi. The best are also minerally and complex.

4.) **Pinot Grigio**—also known as Pinot Gris, not widely grown outside Italy, Alsace, and the U.S., mainly Oregon, good acidity, low alcohol, can be pale, even with hints of pink, and muted both in nose and mouth. When treated with respect, as in Alsace, it tends to deeper color and a richer, slightly spicy, honeyed character.

5.) **Sémillon**—at its best in the Bordeaux region of France, a small amount is grown in Australia (of very good quality), South Africa, the U.S. Can be quite viscous. Dry versions are fresh and citrusy with a hint of nuttiness when young, acquiring a marvelous golden-orangey hue and a waxy, butterscotch quality with age. It's as a dessert wine, however, infected with noble rot (the fungus Botrytis cinerea that concentrates the grapes' sugars) that Sémillon reaches its highest expression.

6.) **Chenin Blanc**—France, South Africa, made in every style from bone-dry to sweet dessert, aggressive acidity but with surprising fullness and texture, very long-lived, best enjoyed within a couple of years of vintage or after 10 years or more, shows more mineral and flowers than fruit, tremendous complexity when mature.

7.) **Gewürztraminer**—Alsace, Italy, Germany, Austria, Canada, U.S., a wine you either love or don't, hugely aromatic. The best have gigantic aromas of roses, orange blossom, spices, perfume. Very viscous, medium coppery-yellow color, could sometimes use more acid, a dramatic, enticing varietal when well made.

8.) **Grüner Veltliner**—Austria, Austria, and Austria, aka "Groovy," undergoing a surge in popularity, pale-yellow with greenish highlights, high acidity, good mouth feel, a bit peppery, may show lentil or green pea, citrus, or honey; a wine-bar favorite.

9.) **Albariño**—Spain, Portugal, wonderfully light, good acidity and alcohol, apricots, citrus, white peach, quite aromatic, can finish with a touch of bitterness.

10.) **Viognier**—all about the aromatics, France, Australia, U.S., high alcohol, low acidity, full-bodied, effusive, perfumey nose of violets, peaches, apricot, very floral, best enjoyed within a year of release.

THE MOST-LIKELY-TO-ENCOUNTER RED VARIETIES

1.) **Cabernet Sauvignon**—the king of varietals, France, Italy, U.S., Australia, Chile, and to some degree nearly everywhere else, likes good sunlight, can be bold or elegant, medium- to full-bodied, dark-hued, excellent tannic structure, good aromas, black currant, black cherry, dark berries, hints of graphite, cedar, cigar box, mint, green pepper, immensely popular and widespread.

2.) **Pinot Noir**—traditionally about elegance and delicacy, France, U.S. (California, Oregon), Australia, at its best in cooler climes, lighter-hued, has noticeable acidity, light- to medium-bodied, perfumey, barnyard, red fruit and spice, supple mouth feel, rich flavors, cherry, strawberry, blackberry, tea.

3.) **Merlot**—plush, fleshy, the "second" red grape of Bordeaux and much of the world, dark color, moderate tannins, tends toward the low end of the acidity scale, very fruity, plums, cocoa, even a touch earthy, known for its velvety, silky texture.

4.) **Syrah/Shiraz**—*Syrah* in its French homeland, *Shiraz* in South Africa, Australia, and either one in South America, U.S. and the rest of the world; deep-hued, brooding, big-shouldered, big tannins, full-bodied, can have gorgeous, almost flowery aromas, shows meaty black-pepper notes, rich, dark fruit, chocolate, a succulent, characterful mouth feel.

5.) **Sangiovese**—the "blood of Jove," Italy's most widely planted red grape, medium-hued, develops an orangey rim, lovely fresh flavors of red cherry, sour cherry, cranberries, a bit of earthiness, tea and spices, even suggestions of chocolate and orange on the finish, great acidity, an ideal food wine.

6.) **Zinfandel**—quintessentially Californian, kissing cousin to Italian Primitivo, usually good tannins and acidity. Often with very high alcohol, so balance and sweetness can be problems. Dark-hued, bursting with raspberries, blackberries, cinnamon, baking spices, even prunes or raisins. Enjoy young.

7.) **Tempranillo**—Spain's main squeeze, goes by half a dozen regional names, also in Portugal, Argentina, deep-colored, neither overly alcoholic nor tannic, can have lovely aromatics, raspberries, dark cherries, cocoa, coffee, tobacco, plums, commonly oak-aged, adding vanilla, dill and spice notes.

8.) **Nebbiolo**—icon of Piedmont, northern regions of Italy, produces some of the world's greatest wines, hugely tannic, acidic, needs age to soften and reach its drinking peak, complex, distinctive nose, roses, cherries, tar, forest floor, leather, mushrooms, exotic, powerful.

9.) **Cabernet Franc**—the cool-climate Cabernet, Bordeaux and the Loire Valley in France, Italy, U.S., Chile, New Zealand; spicy, violets, raspberry, medium color and body, often used as a blender, lithe and tasty, tends to leanness in cooler vintages.

10.) **Garnacha/Grenache**—*Garnacha* in its homeland of Spain, *Cannonau* in Sardinia, *Grenache* in France, Australia and elsewhere; juicy, flashy, high alcohol, low tannins and acidity, likes warm weather and dry soil, may show pepper, coffee and olives along with distinct raspberry, strawberry, black currant, not for long aging, also makes excellent rosé.

11.) **Gamay**—only major grape vinified primarily by the carbonic maceration process, a hallmark of modern Beaujolais. Bright purplish-red, low tannin, high acid, light- to medium-bodied, aromas and flavors of raspberry, strawberry, bubble gum, bananas, works well as a warm-weather quaffing wine.

12.) **Malbec**—aka *Côt* or *Auxerrois*, originally a blending grape in Bordeaux, main varietal in Cahors (also in France), has found worldwide acclaim in Argentina, dark, almost black-hued, good acid, prominent tannins, lush, fruity, mulberry, blackberry, violets.

This section could go on for hundreds of pages, as there are literally thousands of grape varieties used to make wine in various parts of the world. Even the experts regularly come across grape types they've never heard of. And not only haven't they heard of them, but they often can't tell whether the grapes produce red wines or white.

As a newcomer to the world of wine, never feel embarrassed or lacking in knowledge because someone throws an unknown wine or grape name at you. Just tell them that you've never tasted that particular varietal and ask where the grape comes from and how it might best be described. In the end, that's how we all learn.

The grape varieties listed and briefly described above will cover the bulk of what you'll encounter. Now when a bottle says *Malbec* or *Merlot* or *Pinot Noir*, you'll have an idea of what to expect. If the varietal name isn't on the wine's front label, look on the back. Wines, especially blended wines, will often give you grape types and percentages on the bottle's back label.

New World wines are usually identified by varietal, making your task easier. However, for many wines from Spain, France, Italy and other regions, the wine name may have nothing to do with the grapes within. The section that follows provides an alphabetical list of common wine names and the grape varieties they comprise. So read, drink, and be merry!

COMMON WINES AND THEIR VARIETAL COMPONENTS

- **Amarone** (Italy)—Corvina, Rondinella, Molinara, dried
- **Barbaresco** (Italy)—Nebbiolo
- **Barolo** (Italy)—Nebbiolo

- **Beaujolais** (France)—Gamay
- **Bordeaux**, Left Bank (red, France)—Cabernet Sauvignon, with Cabernet Franc, Merlot, Petit Verdot
- **Bordeaux**, Right Bank (red, France)—Merlot, with Cabernet Franc, Cabernet Sauvignon
- **Bordeaux** (white, France)—Sémillon, Sauvignon Blanc
- **Brunello di Montalcino** (Italy)—Sangiovese
- **Burgundy** (red, France)—Pinot Noir
- **Burgundy** (white, France)—Chardonnay
- **Cava** (Spain)—Macabeo, Parellada and Xarel-lo
- **Chablis** (France)—Chardonnay
- **Champagne** (France)—Chardonnay, Pinot Noir and/or Pinot Meunier
- **Châteauneuf-du-Pape** (France)—Grenache, Syrah, Mourvèdre, and up to ten other allowable varieties
- **Chianti** (Italy)—Sangiovese, may include a percentage of Canaiolo, Colorino and other minor grapes
- **Chinon** (France)—Cabernet Franc
- **Condrieu** (France)—Viognier
- **Cornas** (France)—Syrah
- **Côte-Rôtie** (France)—Syrah, may contain a small percentage of Viognier
- **Côtes du Rhone** (France)—Grenache, Syrah, varying amounts of Mourvèdre, Carignan, Cinsault, and others
- **Crozes-Hermitage** (France)—Syrah
- **Gavi** (Italy)—Cortese
- **Gigondas** (France)—Grenache, Syrah and/or Mourvèdre and others
- **GSM** (Australia)—Grenache, Syrah, Mourvèdre
- **Hermitage** (France)—Syrah
- **Jumilla** (Spain)—Monastrell, Garnacha
- **Langhe Rosso** (Italy)—Nebbiolo, Barbera and/or Cabernet Sauvignon

- **Meritage** (U.S.)—a Bordeaux-style blend of Cabernet Sauvignon, Merlot, Cabernet Franc, and/or Malbec, Petit Verdot
- **Montepulciano d'Abruzzo** (Italy)—Montepulciano
- **Morellino di Scansano** (Italy)—Sangiovese
- **Port** (Portugal, sweet)—Touriga Francesa, Touriga Nacional, Tinta Roriz, Tinta Barroca, Tinta Cão; up to 80 allowable varietals
- **Pouilly-Fumé** (France)—Sauvignon Blanc
- **Pouilly-Fuissé** (France)—Chardonnay
- **Priorat** (Spain)—Garnacha, Cariñena and/or Cabernet Sauvignon, Syrah
- **Ribera del Duero** (Spain)—Tempranillo and/or Garnacha, Cabernet Sauvignon
- **Rioja** (Spain)—Tempranillo, Garnacha, Graciano, Mazuelo
- **Rosso di Montalcino** (Italy)—Sangiovese
- **Sancerre** (France)—Sauvignon Blanc
- **Sauternes** (sweet, France)—Sémillon, Sauvignon Blanc, Muscadelle
- **Savennières** (France)—Chenin Blanc
- **Sherry** (Spain)—Palomino; Pedro Ximénez for sweet styles
- **Soave** (Italy)—Garganega
- **Taurasi** (Italy)—Aglianico
- **Tokaji** (sweet, Hungary)—Furmint
- **Vacqueyras** (France)—Grenache, Syrah, Mourvèdre and others
- **Valpolicella** (Italy)—Corvina, Rondinella, Molinara
- **Vino Nobile di Montepulciano** (Italy)—Sangiovese
- **Vouvray** (France)—Chenin Blanc

And so many others. But this will provide a good start, whether you want to look for a specific type of wine or discover your own personal favorites.

9

Nickel Tour of the Great Wine Regions Part I: A Little Old World Geography To Make You Look Brilliant

hall we start at the old center of the wine world or the new? Do we even know where the new center is? Some would say the United States, with its established appellations of excellence like Napa and Sonoma, or its exciting newcomers: Oregon, producing what's arguably the best Pinot Noir outside Burgundy, or Washington state, turning out elegant yet powerful Syrahs, Cabernets and Merlots, along with more exotic varietals like Viognier and Lemberger.

Others would claim Italy or Spain as the epicenter, the first for its incredible variety of wine and grape types, many of them exciting, food-friendly and increasingly available, the latter for the consistent upswing in quality and a blossoming of new regions that Spain has experienced during the past twenty years while still preserving traditional varietals and providing exceptional consumer value.

We know Australia has stumbled and is now, thankfully, recovering, and strongly. Portugal's unfortified table wines (i.e., neither Port nor Madeira, but regular dry wines) have shown tremendous improvement but still have a way to go; South Africa seems to take two steps forward followed by another one back. Greece, where in so many ways it all began, is finally realizing that its value lies in its unique and delicious native varietals and not in blending Merlot or Cabernet with everything. And Chile and Argentina, the up-and-comers of Latin America, may be producing serious and remarkably delicious wines, but they're just beginning to affect the international conversation about what direction the wine world should go in.

In fact, when you come right down to it, the old center of all things vinous is still the benchmark. Le France. No way around it. It may be having problems ranging from overpricing to declining consumption to loss of international market share, but no country produces such a variety of top-tier wines year after year after year. And no other country's problems, successes, vintages, personalities, traditions and top wines resonate so compellingly from London to Hong Kong, from Santiago to Sydney to San Francisco. France is still, for better or worse, the country through which all wine discussion must eventually pass. And so ... the countries:

These country vignettes are by no means intended to be complete. Areas are left out, wines are overlooked. But they will provide an excellent introduction to each nation's wine highlights and offer a representative sampling of the best to be had from each of the world's important wine-producing countries.

Don't feel you have to read Chapters 9 and 10 straight through. Though you may wish to do just that, there's no harm in skipping some, or even all, the countries

---

—though there's a lot of great wine info contained
in this survey of regions, not to mention a word
or two about their best beers.

If you like, pick your favorite countries or
the ones you're hoping to visit. Do a little daydreaming;
after all, there's no exam at the end of the book. You can
return to the others at any time, as often as you like.

FRANCE

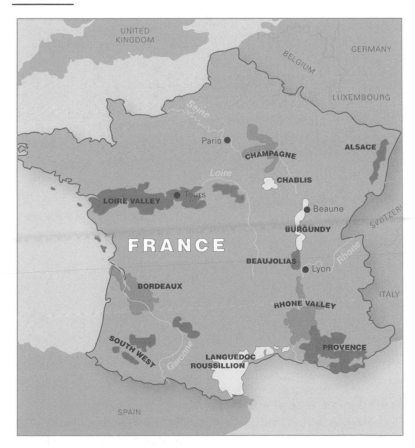

A centuries-long tradition has established standards that still define excellence. France is home to Champagne, where the world's finest sparkling wines are made; Bordeaux, site of the world's most compelling Cabernet- and Merlot-based and blended wines; Burgundy, the essential, the heart and soul of Pinot Noir; Northern Rhone, ancestral home and highest expression of Syrah; Southern Rhone, home of Grenache-based wines extraordinaire; and any number of secondary regions, including the Loire Valley, Alsace, and Languedoc-Roussillon, that in and of themselves could define the entire wine culture of any number of smaller countries. Not to mention a whole panoply of world-class sweet wines and, oh, yes, some of the most delicious rosés anywhere.

How did the French get so good at this? First, after the fall of the Roman Empire, the church owned and controlled most vineyards. The monks who ran these early wine estates kept meticulous written records and over the years determined which grapes did best, insofar as producing superior wine, in which very specific areas. Hence the French connection to the concept, and importance, of *terroir*.

Second, by the early 1200s, wine was being shipped to England and other points outside their areas of origin. To maintain the integrity—and profits—of this commerce, rigorous wine laws were established to standardize and protect the reputation of their product.

What results is a thousand-plus years of wine study and cultivation, official church and government sanction and support, a wine-friendly climate, extensive weather, soil and site observation and insight, cheap labor, and growing markets, both domestic and international, for their product. It would have been amazing had they not succeeded.

Wines To Try, Regions To Explore
Champagne is the storied product of the Champagne region, some 90 miles northeast of Paris, one of the world's northernmost

winegrowing areas. The sparkling wine is made from grapes grown on chalky soil and is among the most complicated wines to produce. Dozens of individual lots of grapes are fermented and later blended together to create what the winemaker anticipates will be representative of the "house style" of the winery. This *assemblage* is then bottled with yeast and a small amount of sugar and wine and undergoes a second fermentation, resulting in a bottleful of bubbles and a rich, yeasty flavor. Most Champagne is NV, or non-vintage. Try any of the well-known labels, or what's called a "grower Champagne," more like a craft brew, that tends to be a better expression of both *terroir* and vintage. These can be identified by the letters *RM* on the front label.

Well south of Paris, along the banks of the Gironde river as it empties into the Atlantic, one finds both the city and region of Bordeaux. In many opinions, the best wines of this region are simply the best wines. The southern, or Left Bank, is home to the world's greatest, and most expensive, Cabernet Sauvignon blends; the labels to look for generally feature a chateau name over the sub-region or commune, the best being Médoc, Haut-Médoc, St.-Estèphe, Pauillac, St.-Julien, Margaux, Graves and Pessac-Léognan. Not all chateaux are created equal, however. A bottle from Pauillac or Margaux or any of these other areas is no guarantee of fabulous wine. But it does put you in the best neighborhoods!

Bordeaux wines can be tannic, powerful, and too young for maximum enjoyment when first released. These are wines meant to be aged, built for the long haul—though real aficionados will enjoy a bottle or two before cellaring the bulk of their purchase. And like its rival for greatness, Burgundy, these wines are definitely affected by the vagaries of weather. Vintage *is* important and should be considered when making your selection.

Across the river, on the so-called Right Bank, the communes of Pomerol and St.-Emilion bear the standard for the world's top Merlot-based wines. These tend to be a bit fatter and richer and are approachable sooner than their Cabernet cousins, though, unfortunately, the best are no less expensive.

And lest we move on too quickly, a bit upriver is found the commune of Sauternes. The name alone will make sweet-wine lovers weak in the knees. These wines (also called Sauternes) are made primarily of Sémillon grapes infected with Botrytis cinerea, aka noble rot, a fungus that concentrates their sugars and adds an ethereal taste to the resulting wine. Berries are individually picked, ensuring that only those with the proper amount of fungus become part of the wine. So painstaking and selective is this process that it's often said an individual vine won't yield more than a single glass of wine. A sip of Sauternes can be a transformative experience. If you're rich, look for Chateau d'Yquem. Otherwise, any number of chateaux will fill the bill.

Back to the east, in the middle of the country, is the small but spectacular region of Burgundy, trailing like a path of stars from the south side of Champagne, stopping first in Chablis. Here are to be found the most electric, minerally Chardonnays in France's still-wine category. As with everything in this region, look for 1er (Premier) Cru and Grand Cru to specify wines of the best vineyards. Once further south, one finds the Cote d'Or, the golden slopes, the heart of Burgundy. Comprising hundreds of small holdings, some no more than a few rows of the best vineyards, this is an area where the novice is better off knowing a few respected producer names or the best villages. Also realize that 99% of the stunning wines of Burgundy are the product of only two grapes: Pinot Noir for the reds and Chardonnay for the whites.

These are the ultimate expression of *terroir*, each vineyard, each individual site, lending its own peculiarities. From north to south, and with a willing pocketbook, look for reds from Gevrey-Chambertin, Morey-St.-Denis, Vougeot, Echezeaux, Vosne-Romanée, Nuits-St.-Georges, Aloxe-Corton, Pommard,

Volnay, and Santenay, and whites from Aloxe-Corton, Meursault, Puligny-Montrachet, Chassagne-Montrachet, and Rully.

The producers that can be depended on include Bouchard Père & Fils, Maison Joseph Drouhin, Domaine Jean Grivot, Maison Louis Jadot, Henri Jayer, Domaine des Comtes Lafon, Domaine Leflaive, Domaine Leroy, Domaine Méo-Camuzet, Domaine Denis Mortet, and the Holy Grail, Domaine de la Romanée-Conti. Confusing? Absolutely. Welcome to Burgundy. It often disappoints, being so dependent on vintage and producer. But when this appellation excels, it produces the finest Pinot Noirs and the most gorgeous Chardonnays the world has to offer. Take a flier; you just might get lucky.

Not to be overlooked is Beaujolais, just south of Burgundy, and its fruity, often simple Gamay-based wines, the best of which take the names of their villages. The Cru Beaujolais, the best of the region, are led by wines labeled Morgon, Moulin-à-Vent, and Juliénas. These are light- to medium-bodied reds, inexpensive, and perfect for a picnic or aperitif. It seems the Gamay grape is one that people either enjoy greatly or have little use for. Try these wines; after all, the objective is to find what *you* like to drink, even if it's lager light.

Continuing south, we again run into world-class wines (these French just don't quit!) in the spectacular Rhône Valley. The Northern Rhône is a series of tiny appellations hugging steep slopes above the Rhône river: Côte-Rôtie and Hermitage, deservedly the two most renowned sources of exquisite Syrah; Cornas and St. Joseph, not far behind, and Crozes-Hermitage, thankfully a bit more affordable. This is also home to the world's greatest Viogniers, from the vineyards of Condrieu and Chateau Grillet. Following the river south until it opens into a broad rocky plain, the Southern Rhône offers rich, powerful reds from Chateauneuf-du-Pape, Gigondas, Vacqueyras and the Côte du Rhone Villages, Grenache-based wines usually incorporating various percentages of Syrah, Mourvèdre, and possibly Cinsaut and Carignan (or, in the case of Chateauneuf-du-Pape, up to thirteen allowable varietals).

As if this remarkable selection of fine wine weren't enough, don't miss the rosés of Provence; the earthy reds of the Mediterranean coast, from Marseille to the Spanish border (the Languedoc-Roussillon); the fabulous Sauvignon Blancs of Sancerre and Pouilly-Fumé and the Chenin Blancs of Savennières and Vouvray, in the Loire Valley; or the unctuous, fruity Pinot Gris, Rieslings, and Gewürztraminers of Alsace. So much wine, so little time.

France: Best Beer Bets
The diversity of France's wine holdings hasn't spilled over to its beer industry. Large breweries control over 90% of the market. The best-known may be Kronenbourg, and its most popular brew, Kronenbourg 1664, is a rather good lager with a nice taste of malt. But the beers to go after are the *bieres de garde*, a traditional farmhouse style brewed in winter and spring, with a spicy hops influence balanced by a good dose of malt, 6.5% to 8.5% alcohol, deep blond to red brown, and almost ale-like. The top names to look for are 3 Monts, Jenlain and Ch'ti.

ITALY

France and Italy consistently run neck and neck for the title of No. 1 producer of fine wine. While France has many great wine-producing regions, Italy is more akin to one huge vineyard, with different grape types planted in different sections. To the Italians, wine is a food, an integral part of dining, whether as part of a simple lunch or an elaborate dinner. Italian wines are food wines, meaning they tend to have a higher level of mouth-watering acidity and are at their best in the company of something delicious to eat.

Wines To Try, Regions To Explore

Barolos and Barbarescos from the northern region of Piedmont are glorious, powerful wines, both 100% Nebbiolo and best with a few years of age. For something to drink now, at much less expense, try any of the very good Barberas or juicy Dolcettos from the same area. Also from the north, from Veneto, don't overlook Valpolicella or the amazingly rich, velvety Amarones, made from the same trio of Corvina, Rondinella, and Molinara grapes. And while in the neighborhood of Venice and gondolas and grand old *palazzi,* look for Prosecco, made from the Glera grape, possibly Italy's favorite sparkling wine, more fizz than bubbles, made dry or slightly sweet, with soft nutty flavors, a bit lemony, and a favorite at cafés along the Grand Canal.

Chiantis, composed primarily of Sangiovese but with other grapes allowed, are practically the signature Italian wine in the U.S., but try a magnificent Brunello di Montalcino, also from Tuscany and of a different clone of Sangiovese, the lesser Rosso di Montalcino, or the Sangiovese-based wines from the newer Maremma district. As to the so-called Super Tuscans, that designation has lost much of its original cachet and simply means the producer has chosen not to follow rules that would allow the wine to be labeled *Chianti.* Super Tuscans are often blends incorporating Cabernet Sauvignon or Merlot along with Sangiovese, though just about any mix is possible. These wines can be either fabulous or very ordinary.

As one moves south, the wines take on a richer, darker, cooked-fruit, fig-and-date quality. Many of the grapes were brought here by the Greeks and have a two thousand-year history. Look for Aglianico in the Basilicata and Campania regions (del Vultures are wonderful, and the pricey Taurasi, when good, are stunning). Try the Negroamaro and Primitivo (an Italian offshoot of the Zinfandel family) wines of Puglia, and don't overlook Sicily's major red, Nero d'Avola.

And the whites! From north to south, crisp, distinct, often with a touch of bitter almond on the finish, a taste near and dear to Italian palates. For a good sampling, start with the Gavis, of Piedmont, made from the Cortese grape, often merely crisp and lean but in good vintages showing red apple, honey, even floral notes; the gorgeous white blends of Alto-Adige and Friuli, complex wines comprising Chardonnay, Pinot Grigio, Pinot Bianco, Gewurztraminer, and/or Sauvignon Blanc; and Soave, the reasonably priced expression of Garganega grapes, fruity and dry, and, like the easy-to-drink Prosecco, also from the Veneto. Moving south, look for Vernaccia (di San Gimignano if possible), with its full body and honeyed, earthy flavors; Verdicchio, a white that can actually take some aging of its citrusy, appley notes; and Fiano di Avellino and Greco di Tufo, speaking of Greek imports, both nutty with hints of stone fruit, perfect with almost any simply prepared seafood.

Italy: Best Beer Bets

As in France, much beer is drunk in Italy, especially by the younger crowd not so tied to the wine mentality as their elders. But unlike its neighbor, Italy has a growing and quite exciting craft beer scene that's highly regarded by those in the know. In the Veneto, Audace Golden Ale layers herbal, peppery notes over a nice malty base while Lombardy is home to Birrificio di Como, and Piedmont—perhaps the center of Italy's beer renaissance—claims Birreria Menabrea along with Birrificio Baladin and its well known brands Elixir and Super Baladin, interesting takes on strong Belgian ale. Still, in much of Italy the old standbys are the best bets and include the tasty Peroni, and its premium offering, Nastro Azzurro, and the well-made if uninspiring Moretti.

SPAIN

Ah, Spain. Intense and beautiful. Visit a bistro in France or Italy and you'll probably find only the wine or wines of the local region; stop in for a drink or a bite to eat at the humblest of establishments in Spain and chances are you'll be offered a selection of wines from every corner of the country. There's a pride in Spain that celebrates all its wines. Certainly there are conflicts and rivalries among various regions, but when the subject is wine, it seems cooperation replaces competition.

In the past twenty years, this ancient wine culture (established by the Phoenicians over three thousand years ago) has risen from a decades-long slumber, shaken off its practice of oak-aging wine for so many years that there was little left but the hard taste of wood, cleaned up its production techniques, gained new respect for the flavors and character of its native varietals, rediscovered the pleasures of fresh, crisp whites, and stepped boldly and successfully into the modern wine world. And not at the expense of anything worth saving, like the glory and uniqueness of Sherry or the vast tracts of wizened, hundred-year-old vines or the lovely, familiar flavors of red fruit and vanilla that result from aging the Tempranillo-based wines of Rioja in American oak.

Spain has more acreage planted to vineyards than any other country, though because many are low-yielding old vines, it ranks only third in total production behind France and Italy. And yet it's these same old vines, struggling in poor soils that make for the best, most complex wines. Indeed, Spain is a storehouse of great traditional varieties that continue to define its wine styles and character. As well, this country has no lack of visionaries. Even as they've maintained the best of the old, new vineyards and new regions have sprung up as improved techniques and discoveries of favorable microclimates have expanded Spain's number of designated wine regions, its DOs (for *Denominación de Origen*), from 54 in 1999 to 70 in 2009.

■ *TECHNICAL DRIVEL* ■

Spanish law still classifies wines largely by how long they're aged. While there are minor differences from region to region, in much of Spain the progression begins with

- **Crianza,** wine made from good but not exceptional grapes and aged for two years, at least one of which must be in barrel, producing fruit-forward, easy-drinking wines for everyday consumption.
- **Reservas,** usually of better-quality grapes and aged a minimum of three years, one of which must be in barrel, creating a richer, more robust wine combining the flavors of higher-tier fruit with the maturation and seasoning of oak barrels.
- **Gran Reserva,** aged at least five years, with no less than two in barrel. Formerly the pinnacle of the Spanish wine pyramid, some Gran Reservas are falling out of favor as the trend is more toward the flavors of plums and berries and fruit and less to the leather and tobacco influences of extended wood aging.

In any case, a significant difference between Spanish producers and those in the rest of the world is that minimum requirements for aging are often exceeded. Unlike many vintners trying to get their wines bottled and out the door as quickly as the rules allow—either for economic reasons or simply to make room for the next vintage—Spaniards have a tradition of not releasing any wine until they believe it's ready to drink, regardless of the time and expense involved. This care for the finished product is certainly one more reason to give the wines of Spain the attention they deserve.

Wines To Try, Regions To Explore

Without question, Spain's best-known wine region is La Rioja, and its wines are still among the best in the country. These Tempranillo-based beauties are often but not always blended with Garnacha for more body and alcohol, Mazuelo for deeper color, and Graciano to enhance the aromatics and elegance. Historically aged for upwards of ten or fifteen years, their traditional style is one of depth and complexity, of leather and spice and a supple richness. Even in more modern versions, however, wood-aged for no more than a year or two, Riojas have an earthy vibrancy that matches perfectly with the foods of the region— mushrooms and garlic, potatoes and chorizo, roast lamb with slow-cooked peppers and tomatoes.

Just to the east, toward the French border, lies the DO Navarra, where, in addition to the Rioja varietals and the region's well-known rosados (rosés), some of the country's best experiments with the international grapes Cabernet Sauvignon and Merlot and Chardonnay are being bottled. Continuing toward Barcelona takes one past Penedès, the heart of Spain's cava industry. Cavas, the world's top-selling sparkling wines, are made in the same way as Champagne but using Parellada, Macabeo, and Xarel-lo grapes. The good ones are delicious, and almost all are inexpensive. But this region isn't just cava; in fact, one of Spain's premier wines, the Torres "Mas La Plana," 100% Cabernet Sauvignon, hails from Penedès.

Nearby is Montsant, a source for great bold, tasty reds also at relatively low cost. But the force of nature in this corner of Catalonia, almost hiding within Montsant, is the tiny, magnificent Priorat. This ancient area of steep, rocky slopes and a unique granite and slate soil called *licorella* produces some of the most powerful, profound, dense, complex, high-quality wines found anywhere. They can be expensive, but the massive body and flavors of these predominantly Garnacha and Cariñena wines are well worth the price of admission.

South along the Mediterranean, the regions of Yecla and Jumilla are producing good to outstanding Monastrells, the grape known in France as Mourvèdre. And finally, in the far south of Andalucía, a stone's throw from North Africa, is the home of Sherry, among the world's most varied, complex and least understood types of wine.

Sherry is vinified primarily from the Palomino grape, with sweeter versions also utilizing Pedro Ximénez, or PX, grapes. Grown in the chalky *albariza* soils around Jerez, Sherries range from bone-dry, delicate, and exceedingly pale in color to huge, dark and thick as molasses sweet wines. As Sherry is fortified after fermentation, all versions are high in alcohol, ranging from 15 ½% to 22%. The pale, dry versions—fino and manzanilla— are tangy and fragile with flavors of almonds and mushrooms and a taste of the sea, best served chilled to accompany tapas and seafood. Amontillados are simply finos aged to ten years or more, showing a richer, fuller palate, darker in color. All three styles are influenced by the *flor*, a blanket of yeast that grows over the wine, both protecting it from too much oxygen and letting it slowly take on some character of oxidation. The other major style of Sherries is darker, richer, more pungent and oxidized, with increasing notes of caramel, figs, licorice and dried fruits, and includes palo cortado, a bridge between the two groups; oloroso, sometimes dry, often sweetened with the addition of small amounts of PX; cream Sherries, quite sweet, rich and delicious, with at least 15% PX; and 100% Pedro Ximénez, a wine that pours like syrup, that's black as night, a cauldron of toffee, dried cherries, walnuts, chocolate, dates and brown sugar, among the world's richest and sweetest dessert wines.

All Sherries pass through the age-old solera system, where vintages have no meaning. As wine to be bottled is drawn off from the oldest barrels, the same amount is taken from the next oldest to top off the first, and so on, up the line through six or ten or fourteen rows of barrels to those holding the youngest wine, the current vintage.

The result is a bottling that is a complex blend of dozens of years, and the reason Sherry isn't vintage dated—though some producers put the year the solera was first begun on their labels, which may date back to the 1800s.

Leaving the land of dry, arid hills, of flamenco and bullfighting, we hop over much of central Spain to the region just north of Portugal, to the green lushness of Galicia and its crisp, lemony, peachy Albariños. The leading area for this fresh and refreshing white is the DO Rías Baixas. Heading inland along the Duero River is Toro, producing increasingly good Tempranillo (here called Tinto de Toro), and Rueda, a premier white wine region, and then, a few hours north of Madrid, the important and influential DO of Ribera Del Duero. Some of the best of Spain's reds, concentrated, structured, and yet with excellent fruit, primarily Tempranillo (they say Tinto Fino or Tinto del País here) and Cabernet Sauvignon, come from this historic region, and should not be missed.

Spain: Best Beer Bets

The *cervecería* is an important part of Spanish nighttime food and drink culture. While many patrons have a glass of wine with their tapas and later with dinner, others opt for a *caña*, a draft beer served in very small glasses and a good way to experience various regional brews while you're traveling. Otherwise, look for Mahou, Estrella Galicia, Estrella Damm, or any of the Alhambra brand. And should you be in Asturias or the Basque country of northern Spain, a great experience is drinking (and pouring) the traditional hard cider called *sidra*. Servers hold the bottle two or three feet above the glasses and direct a thin stream into each glass, aerating the cider and testing their aim at the same time.

PORTUGAL

Diminutive heavyweight in the world of wine. Barely 125 miles wide and only 370 miles from north to south, Portugal is home to two of the world's most famous and highly regarded fortified wines and an increasing number of surprisingly good table wines. It may also be the country that has held most firmly to its lineup of traditional varietals, grapes that for the most part are found nowhere else.

Wines To Try, Regions To Explore

In deference to history and fame, a serious look at the wines of Portugal should begin with Port. Perhaps the most lauded—unquestionably the best known—of dessert wines, Port is a fortified wine, meaning that a measure of brandy or other grape spirit is added during the latter stages of fermentation, killing the remaining yeast and leaving a significant measure of residual sugar, an age-old technique originally developed to stabilize and preserve wines that were transported by ship in the days of sail and before refrigeration. The resulting wine is rich, full-bodied, high in alcohol and deliciously sweet. It's made in the Douro

113

region of northern Portugal from as many as 80 different indigenous grape varieties, grown on steep, mountainous terraces.

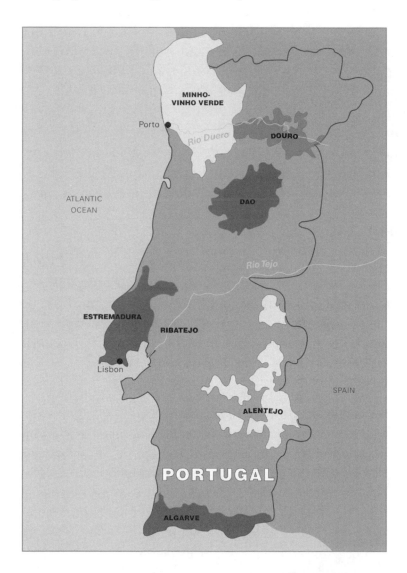

When the wine-loving gentry of England found themselves in the midst of various wars and diplomatic face-offs with the French, their usual source of good-quality grape juice, in the 17th,

18th and 19th centuries, they turned to regions like Spain and Portugal to fill the gap. Port was an early mainstay, so beloved by certain English merchants that they moved to the region and established their own shipping companies. Hence the number of English names among the best of the Port producers, which list would include Cockburn's, Croft, Dow's, Fonseca, Graham's, Niepoort, Quinta do Noval, Ramos Pinto, Sandeman, Taylor Fladgate, and Warre's. For simple, straightforward after-dinner drinking, a ruby Port is tasty and inexpensive. Much more compelling, though, is an aged tawny Port, set aside in cask for 10, 20, even 30 or 40 years before being bottled and released, ready to be enjoyed. The extended aging accounts for the deep golden, tawny color and the scrumptious, nutty flavors of caramel, brown sugar, and vanilla. At the top of the heap are the vintage Ports, labeled as such and produced only in the best years. Rather than undergoing lengthy aging in wood, vintage Ports spend two years in barrel and are released to be bottle-aged by the buyer for another 10, 20, or 30+ years. These wines are magnificent, complex, about power and layers of flavor rather than delicacy, and one of wine-drinking's great pleasures.

While still in the Douro or the neighboring region of the Dao, also look for the red blends of those same names. As in much of Europe, most of Portugal's wines are named for their regions of origin rather than for the grapes they contain. A good thing, too, at least in this repository of varietals like Alfrocheiro Preto, Bastardo, Baga, Tinta Barroca, Tinta Roriz, Tinto Cão, Touriga Nacional, and Touriga Francesa—and those are merely a sampling of the red wine grapes. The wines they're blended to produce tend to be on the rustic side, with a richness and intensity of flavor, perhaps containing a dash of spicy pepperiness.

From powerful reds to a lightweight white, although a thoroughly enjoyable one, look just to the north and west for one of Portugal's iconic Vinho Verdes, a slightly spritzy, low-alcohol wine meant to be drunk very young, the perfect companion to a simple fish dish or a bowl of steamed clams. In the southern half of the country lies Portugal's largest province, the Alentejo, home to numerous wine cooperatives as well as the large, very good producer Esporão. Reds here are made from Periquita, Aragonez (like Tinta Roriz, a clone of Tempranillo), Trincadeira and a large handful of other varietals. Whether from north or south, additional producers and labels worth trying include Aveleda, Quinta do Crasto, Quinta do Côtto, Quinta do Vale Meão, Quinta do Vale D. Maria, Luis Pato, and numerous others pushing the quality envelope.

Lying 500 miles offshore, closer to Africa than Europe, is the small volcanic island of Madeira, home to the marvelous wine of the same name. And please—we're not talking about that nasty brownish stuff found on supermarket shelves for cooking. Real Madeiras are rich and complex, tawny amber in color, fortified to as high as 20% alcohol, with a spine of acidity supporting flavors of toffee, caramel, and orange peel, and ranging from dry Sercial through increasing levels of sweetness—Verdelho, Bual— and finally, to the richest and sweetest of all, Malmsey. Their unique production process includes actually cooking the wine at low temperature, followed by extensive aging and exposure to oxygen, resulting in a characterful, long-lived wine. The flavors are distinctive; not everyone will enjoy them. But these are delicious, comforting wines to legions of drinkers, so give them a try—that's how we learn.

Portugal: Best Beer Bets

Unicer Brewing, outside the city of Porto, makes Portugal's #1 selling brew, Super Bock, distributed widely, including in the U.K., Canada, Spain and the U.S. It comes in Classic, a 5.6% ABV lager, Abadia, a 6.4% ABV dark wheat beer, a supposedly not bad stout, and two varieties of pils: Green, containing lemon flavor, and Tango, with red-currant flavor. Other major players are Sagres, perhaps "the" beer of Lisbon, and Coral, made in Madeira but available throughout the country. Portugal, though, is about wine; don't expect anything stunning in your mug of suds.

GERMANY

Although images of low-quality, sugary, blue-bottled Liebfraumilch constitute the sum total of what many people know about German wine, in fact this cool-climate nation of beer drinkers produces some of the world's most exceptional white wines. Many connoisseurs consider Riesling to be the most noble of all white grapes, and nowhere is it the source of more exciting, nervy, long-lived wines than in Germany. It's remarkable that wine is produced here at all, though it has been since Roman times. Many of its best vineyards are so far north that they exist only by facing due south, on wildly steep slopes hanging directly over either the Mosel or Rhine river, absorbing whatever extra sunlight they can reflected off the water.

And it's not all whites. German winemakers are paying more attention to cool climate reds than ever before. Dornfelder, with its dark, plumy flavors is increasingly popular and one shouldn't overlook some legitimate pockets of Pinot Noir production. But still and all, this is Riesling country.

Thanks to Riesling's unique profile, it makes excellent wine even without fully ripening, a great characteristic in a region as far north as Germany. Expect a lightning bolt of acidity, low alcohol, almost-electric flavors of lime and slate and a racy minerality. These wines range from bone-dry to lusciously sweet. The best are classified on a scale of the grapes' ripeness at harvest. In the more southerly regions—everything is relative—the wines still exhibit that verve common to German whites but have a bit more body and fruit and floral accents.

These are "pure" wines, without oak, without manipulation. They express the slate soils and the high, thin northern sun and have what is called transparency, a quality of tension and elegance. All of which probably sounds like so much hooey—until you drink them! The vibrant flavors and minerality of these wines, like sucking stones and chips of slate dipped in lime and lychee juice, have won over more than one experienced palate. Throw in some schnitzel and red cabbage and you'll have a taste sensation that's hard to beat.

Choose wines labeled *QmP*, meaning *"Qualitätswein mit Prädikat,"* high-quality wine with special attributes—the highest level in the German hierarchy. Below this, often far below, are *QbA* wines, definitely second tier, and best tried only from the top producers.

The German quality scale, based on ripeness level, starting with the least ripe:

- *Kabinett* (look for the term on the label), an off-dry wine.
- *Spätlese*, made from late-harvest, fully ripened grapes, its piercing acidity balanced by a small percentage of residual sugar.
- *Auslese* is made from very ripe grapes, producing a sweet, lush wine.
- *Beerenauslese* (BA), a rich, dessert-style wine made with grapes infected by noble rot, *Botrytis cinerea*.
- *Trockenbeerenauslese* (TBA), the rarest of all, produced only in the finest—i.e., longest and warmest—vintages, the German answer to French Sauternes and one of the world's rarest and richest dessert wines.
- *Eiswein,* made from frozen grapes picked well into winter. The grapes are quickly pressed and the concentrated juice poured off and fermented into a near—ethereal nectar.

Other useful terms are *Trocken* and *Halbtrocken*, meaning "dry" and "half- or almost dry," respectively. If you prefer your Riesling dry, as many do, look for these terms in addition to the quality levels listed above when scanning labels. In certain regions and vintages, wines up to and including *Spätlese* can be made in a dry style.

Even Germans are starting to prefer their wines drier than in the past. Another label indication of dryness is the relatively new term *Selection*, roughly equivalent to *Trocken*.

Wines To Try, Regions To Explore

Along the banks of the Mosel River in what used to be called the Mosel-Saar-Ruwer wine region lie vineyards so steep the vines appear to grow from the faces of the cliffs. It's a miracle

119

of determination that anyone would actually farm these slippery slate-covered hillsides. And yet Mosel Rieslings may well be the greatest in the world. As in Burgundy, vineyards and villages and producers are all-important; look for wines from the towns of Bernkastel (the suffix *er* indicates "from" in German, so *Bernkasteler* would be the labeling), Brauneberg, Graach, Piesport, Urzig, Wehlen, and Zeltingen, or from winemakers Dr. Loosen, Egon Muller-Scharzhof, Fritz Haag, JJ Prum, and St. Urbans-Hof, among others. And if you see *Sonnenhur* on the label, you'll know the grapes are from one of the sunniest, best-sited vineyards along the river.

The Rheingau region, a bit farther east but at about the same latitude, has an even longer history of producing top-quality Riesling. Here the slopes along the less-convoluted banks of the Rhine River are stretched out and gentler and give their grapes access to more sunlight. These wines are rounder and richer, without the piercing sharpness and precision of Mosel Riesling. There's still wonderful acidity, and here it balances suggestions of apricots and honeysuckle. Top villages are Erbach, Geisenheim, Hochheim, Johannisberg, Kiedrich, and Rauenthal. Producers of note include August Eser, Franz Kunstler, Josef Leitz, Schloss Johannisberg, Schloss Vollrads, and Robert Weil. The Rheingau also produces more than credible Spätburgunder (Pinot Noir), mainly from vineyards around the village of Assmannshausen. Look for these from Franz Kunstler and the easy-for-*you*-to-say Staatsweingut Assmannshausen.

Now head south, following the Rhine toward the French border, and move a few miles away from the river into the wine region of Pfalz, perhaps the most exciting and innovative of all German wine regions, and certainly the most improved over the last few years. Being drier and sunnier than most of Germany, the Pfalz is known to produce an exceptional quantity of the riper end of the classification scale, especially the sought-after Beerenauslesen and the Botrytis-infected Trockenbeerenauslesen, and also seems more intent on producing great dry Riesling, identifiable by the stand-alone word *Trocken* on the label. One can also find good Spätburgunder as well as Weissburgunder (Pinot Blanc) here. Pfalz whites are full-bodied, even flashy by German standards, and show off rich flavors of melon and ginger and even peaches and cream. For the best of these, seek out Dr. Bürklin-Wolf, Müller-Catoir, Eugen Müller, Christmann, Geheimer Rat Dr. von Bassermann-Jordan, and Josef Biffar. Remember that most of these names will be preceded by *Weingut*, meaning "winery" or "estate of."

Germany: Best Beer Bets

You've gotta be kidding. This is Germany, center of the beer drinker's universe. If you can't find a great brew in Deutschland, you must be unconscious. And if you are, you've probably found too many excellent ones already—and drunk them all! Wine is small potatoes in this nation of breweries and hops lovers. Every town and village has multiple *rathskellers, hierstube, bräuhaus* and *biergartens*, and all you need remember is "Ein bier, bitte," or "a beer, please," to be both welcome and well served.

Don't overlook the *kellerbiers*, or cellar beer, served only in a brewery's own pub or *biergarten*. Unfiltered, unmolested, un-fooled-around-with. Just pure, fresh, and something you can't enjoy outside Germany. As to the other great styles, where to begin? How about:

- **Altbier** (old beer), which predates lager, is top-fermented, a bit darker and always delicious.
- **Bock**, a strong lager with a malty sweetness.
- **Doppelbock**, stronger yet, around 7% ABV, and richer, maltier.
- **Dortmunder export**, a pale lager, not too hoppy, not too malty, some would say "just right."

- **Dunkel** (dark beer) in a variety of styles including Munich, an early type of lager, brewed with a helping of roasted malt.
- **Hefeweizen**, a top-fermented, unfiltered wheat beer distinguished by its yeast, a popular summer quaff.
- **Kölsch**, brewed in Cologne, a crisp, light lager often made with a small percentage of wheat, delicate, even fruity.
- **Märzen**, brewed in the spring, traditionally stored over the summer and served in autumn, amber, rich, with lots of malt.
- **Oktoberfestbier**, lighter than märzen yet full and malty.
- **Helles**, Munich's answer to Pilsner, though light and less bitter, still with a touch of hops.
- **Pilsner**, the original lager, clean and golden with hints of caramel, a dry finish, and a good dose of spicy hops.
- **Schwarzbier**, the darkest of dunkels, bitter and sweet, roasty and malty, in some ways resembles a stout.
- **Weissbier**, flavorful and refreshing wheat beer (see hefeweizen). has a great tart, citrusy element, a very appealing summer brew.

And that's it—no more. This is supposed to be a wine book. I can already hear you barleycorn sophisticates bemoaning my abbreviated descriptions. And asking where's the rauchbier or the gose or the heller bock?

It's right there, in Germany, if you're fortunate enough to get there, or in your local liquor store otherwise. Unlike the beers of some countries, German brews are widely exported to the U.S. But then, you should already know that!

AUSTRIA

While we're in the neighborhood, it would be an oversight to miss Austria, where the history of winemaking and grape-growing predates the Romans. All the vino action is in the eastern half of the country in a wide crescent that hugs the borders with the Czech Republic, Slovakia, Hungary and Slovenia.

In the northernmost region, confusingly called Lower Austria (so-called as it spreads out along the lower Danube), the country's best Grüner Veltliners show a flashy dash of grapefruit, green pea and white pepper, and magnificent dry Rieslings are among the finest produced anywhere. As far as red wines are concerned, look to Burgenland for the best Blaufränkisch, a riot of raspberries and richness with a hefty dash of pepper—a very nice wine—and to Zweigelt for a fruity, spicy, simpler glass of goodness. At times the two may be blended, perhaps with an addition of Cabernet Sauvignon or Merlot for a delightful and complex cuvee. And seek out a top-notch Austrian eiswein (ice wine) for a white-wine dessert experience more subdued, more elegant, more exquisite than almost anything else in the world of sweet wine.

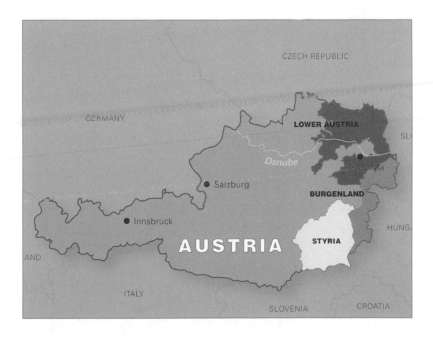

Austria: Best Beer Bets

Austrians love a good time, and a great brew, and have for centuries. It's rumored, with not insubstantial historical foundation, that Mozart himself sucked down a good number of Stiegls in the city of Salzburg. Whether they were Stiegl-Goldbräu or Stiegl-Spezial is open to debate, but both are available to this day. In the west, weissbier is extremely popular, led by Edelweiss Weissbier Hefetrüb. Also big are lagers of various sorts, including märzens, not the same as German märzens but more like a malty Bavarian helles with some hoppiness, pils, dunkels, and full-bodied, bittersweet bockbiers (Weihnachts', to name but one). Look for Gösser, a märzen, in the southern region of Styria, Ottakringer in Vienna, Zipfer Urtyp in Upper Austria, one of the country's best, Weiselburger, Egger, and so many other great beers. And don't forget the city of Pilsen (current Czech name: Plzen) was under Austrian control when lager was first developed. Fortunately, the original brewery where this style of lager, or bottom-fermented beer, was first produced, Pilsner Urquell, is alive and well and its products widely distributed throughout the United States.

GREECE

'The birthplace of Western civilization—and much of the world's wine culture. A land where wine was literally considered a gift from the gods, in this case the son of Zeus, Dionysus. There are said to be more than 300 indigenous varietals in Greece, but as so little Greek wine is exported, knowing just a handful of specific varieties or wine types will suffice. And if you haven't been, and I've not yet had the pleasure, Greece is a country that deserves every wine lover's pilgrimage. Sitting by the dark blue sea under a dazzling bright blue sky with a glass of crisp white or spicy red and a plate of grilled langoustines or octopus or a whole fresh-caught fish or a mound of juicy, charred cubes of pork or sausage or a platter of roast lamb—whew, sounds like an awfully good way to spend a leisurely afternoon.

Wines To Try, Regions To Explore

Should you be in the midst of the Aegean Islands, that glass of white will probably be Assyrtiko (or a blend thereof), grown most notably on the island of Santorini. It has great acid, especially for a warm-weather grape, with gorgeous citrus and mineral notes—but keep an eye peeled for browning and overly mature aromas, as the wine is prone to oxidation. Or should you be in the Peloponnese, perhaps touring the Temple of Zeus or the ruins of Olympia, you may be enjoying one of the country's other outstanding whites, Moschofilero, often dry, sometimes sweet, with floral highlights and a perfect match to much of the local food; or possibly Roditis, a key component in the stony, delicate dry whites of Patras. All these wines, by the way, are widely available in the United States.

And while marveling at the site of the ancient Olympics, you'll want to indulge in the velvety, complex reds of nearby Nemea, one of Greece's two most important red-wine regions, featuring the soft, cherry flavors of the Agiorghitiko grape. Before leaving the Peloponnese, be sure to finish at least one meal with Greece's most famous dessert wine, the fortified red known as Mavrodaphne.

In cutting across central Greece to Athens, you'll be traveling in retsina territory. You may have heard of retsina and dismissed it as a funky imitation of "real" wine, an oddity of Greek culture. In truth, it's probably closer to the wine drunk by the ancients than any other. Large clay vessels, amphorae, were the barrels of antiquity, used to both store and transport wine around the Mediterranean. These tall clay jugs were coated inside and sealed with pine resin to

---

> protect the wine from oxidation. Through the centuries, Greek palates came to enjoy the piney, floral flavors and aromas, though too often in recent years the resin was a mask for poor or faulty winemaking. Nonetheless, there's something exciting about sipping a glass of wine that tastes like much of the world's known wine production tasted in 500 B.C.

From Athens, head north past the plains of Thessaly toward the home of the gods, Mt. Olympus. On the slopes of nearby Mount Vermion, in the heart of ancient Macedonia, lies the AOC of Naoussa. Many consider this the pinnacle of modern Greek wine. Xinomavro is the varietal, a complex, long-lived red that exhibits flavors of olives, spices, red fruit, and tomato. These wines have been compared to Barolos and Burgundies and are not to be missed.

It has become common practice in parts of Greece to blend the so-called international varietals with certain of the indigenous varieties. Don't automatically be put off by an Agiorghitiko-Merlot blend or a bottling of Xinomavro, Cabernet Sauvignon and Syrah. Many of these are well-made, delicious wines that reflect Greece's re-entry into the greater world of wine. Greek winemakers are committed to the marvelous palette of ancient and native grapes at their disposal but, like winemakers everywhere, want to show that they, too, can produce a Cabernet or Chardonnay worthy of competing with the best.

Greece: Best Beer Bets

As might be imagined, the birthplace of enology, of viniculture and viticulture, is far more wine- than beer-oriented. But Greeks do like to party and sing and dance and spend time in local tavernas enjoying life. So there's beer. Much of it European and imported. But fortunately, Greek breweries have stepped up in the past few years. One of the names you'll hear over and over is Mythos, an excellent lager that has become a popular favorite and spawned a new wave of Greek-brewed goodies. Also look for Athenian, a lager with hints of fruit and a clean finish, or Marathon, with a touch of citrus and a sweet aftertaste. Athenian Brewery produces Zorbas, showing malt and grassy hops and a more toasted finish. Another lager to keep your eyes peeled for is Hillas, like many Greek brews a fairly middle-of-the-road though well-made lager. And from Zeos Brewing Company, in the Peloponnese town of Argos, comes Zeos Pilsner and Makedoniki. Surprisingly, a number of these can be found in the U.S., most readily at good Greek restaurants.

■ ■ ■ ■

10

Nickel Tour of the Great Wine Regions Part II: A Little New World Geography To Make You Look Even Smarter

Many of the so-called New World wine regions have been producing wine for scores, if not hundreds, of years. That being so, the obvious question is why they are referred to as "New World."

One reason is to distinguish them from Europe, which should be thought of as "the establishment" of winemaking, hence the "Old World" label (it could as easily be called "old school"). The other reason is to signify their new approach to winemaking, one that's less constrained by rules and regulations and emphasizes the youthful, fruity aspects of wine over the age-induced qualities of leather, tobacco and oxidation.

Research points to the Middle East (Armenia, Iran, Georgia) as the first areas of winemaking. From these breeding grounds, grape-growing and wine knowledge was passed to the Phoenicians, who in turn spread it around the Mediterranean. It was in present-day

France, Italy and Spain that wine became part of both culture and commerce, subject to record-keeping and codification. The result was a highly regulated, tradition-bound industry.

As winemaking took hold outside this sphere, however, there were fewer strictures, and growers were free to adapt new technologies to produce lush, fruit-forward wines for a populace more interested in drinking now, rather than cellaring it for some distant future.

SOUTH AFRICA

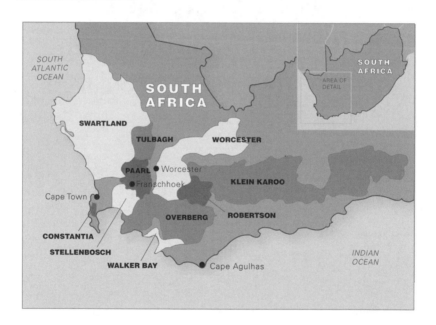

South Africa in many ways straddles the Old World of wine and the New. The first vines, brought from France, Germany, and Spain, were planted in 1655 with the intent of providing food and sustenance to sailors of the Dutch East India Company on their voyages between Europe and the Indies. By the late 1700s, the rich and unctuous sweet wines of Constantia were considered among the world's finest and were a favorite of Napoleon. From there the nation's wine fortunes went into a long decline, though wine has been produced continuously on this southern tip of the African continent since those early days of promise.

The wine regions of South Africa are clustered in the southwest corner of the country, radiating north, south, and east from Cape Town. This is ancient geological territory, built up hundreds of millions of years ago and heavily influenced by currents and climates of two colliding oceans, the Atlantic and the Indian. There are no true indigenous varietals here, as all the vineyards are descendents of those early European cuttings. Despite years of viticultural, economic, and sociological adversity, sometime in the 1980s the wine scene here was transformed by the adoption of modern fermentation techniques and a renewed quest for high quality led by a handful of driven winemakers. So in a sense, South Africa has been producing fine wine for more than 350 years and good wine for about thirty.

The majority of the Cape's vineyards and wineries are clustered in a patchwork quilt of regions and wards and townships that extend some 300 miles east to west and about 400 miles north to south. While one district frequently abuts the next, this chunk of territory is a true panoply of *terroirs* and topographies. Mountains, valleys, slopes, seashores and near-deserts all play a part.

Wines To Try, Regions To Explore

Much of South Africa's grape production is destined for non-wine use like grape concentrate or distillation into brandy or other spirits, but the fine-wine districts that shouldn't be overlooked include Cape Point, Durbanville and Constantia, all lying, almost literally, in the shadow of Cape Town; Stellenbosch, also home to the country's only university program of viticulture and oenology; Paarl and its wards of Wellington and Franschhoek; Robertson; Worcester; and the up-and-coming Walker Bay and Cape Agulhas. None of these locales is more than a two- or two-and-a-half hour drive from Cape Town.

Because of the tremendous diversity of sites and microclimates even within these districts, it makes more sense to discuss the South African wines you'll be most rewarded for trying rather than their specific place of origin.

> The incredibly diverse *terroirs* in South Africa, spawned of its ancient soils, the confluence of the icy-cold Atlantic and the warm Indian oceans and their currents and climatic influences, and thousands of ridges, ripples, slopes, valleys, mountains, and seashores, are also home to the Cape Floral Kingdom, the richest, most diverse plant kingdom on Earth. Considered a World Heritage Site, this area, within which most of the country's grapes are grown, boasts over 9,600 plant species, more than are found in the entire Northern Hemisphere.

Starting with whites, there's nowhere outside the Loire Valley of France that does such an admirable job with Chenin Blanc. From sparkling to sweet dessert styles to off-dry to bone dry, Chenin is almost a signature varietal in South Africa and is, in fact, the country's most widely planted cultivar. When grown with an eye to quality, the result is a high-acid, good-bodied white that shows distinctive notes of honey, peaches, guava and green plum; when overcropped or picked too early, the resultant wine tends to be neutral or boring in flavor and almost harshly acidic.

In days past, the term *steen* was commonly used for Chenin Blanc, often to denote a sweeter style; however, this term has fallen out of favor among many, though not all, winemakers, as it harks back to a time when Chenin quality was secondary to quantity. Even today there seems to be little agreement as to exactly what South African Chenin Blanc should taste like. To a certain degree, this makes exploring the various options an interesting exercise. You may run across a wine showing bright tropical flavors or one hovering around waxy melon and honeysuckle notes. The mouth feel might be viscous or sharp and tart. It's almost a something-for-every-palate kind of proposition. Some consistently good producers to look for are De Trafford, Mulderbosch, Raats, Rudera and Ken Forrester, though by no means should you limit yourself to these labels. Nearly everyone in South Africa makes Chenin Blanc of one style or another.

Sauvignon Blanc is another grape deftly handled here. The best of South Africa's offerings—and they are delicious—combine the flinty, herbal minerality of French Sancerre or Pouilly-Fume with the bracing acidity and tropical and green pepper notes of New Zealand. One can enjoy an almost-endless succession of high-quality, reasonably priced Sauvignon Blancs. The very best hail from the cooler coastal regions and higher-elevation vineyards in a number of the Cape's wine regions. Look for bottlings from producers Groote Post, Vergelegen, Mulderbosch, Thelema, Flagstone, Fleur du Cap, and Nederberg.

If we add to that list Hamilton Russell, Warwick Estate, Meerlust, Rustenberg, Neil Ellis, and perhaps Bouchard Finlayson and Glen Carlou we'll have a list of terrific Chardonnay producers. And South African Chardonnay is delightful; like so many of the country's wines, it combines the best of Old World character—i.e., complexity, elegance, a bit of minerality—with the power and overt fruit of more typically New World versions. The Chards here really are their own expression of South Africa's unique and multifaceted *terroirs* and easily stand with the best from almost anywhere.

In the world of red wine, there's no shortage of good if not stunning Merlot, most of it well priced. If you're a Merlot drinker, you might be surprised at how tasty and well made much of it is. But it's the Cabernet Sauvignons and Syrahs of South Africa that really shine. You'll also find that many of the best reds come from Stellenbosch, unlike the best whites, which tend to hail from a wider diversity of regions. Of course, the handful of high-quality Pinot Noirs, in particular those from Bouchard Finlayson and Hamilton Russell, are sourced mainly from the cool, coastal vineyards of Walker Bay.

Before delving further into the outstanding Cabs and Syrahs, we should take a minute to discuss a uniquely South African "product," the Pinotage grape. And while it's true that there are no indigenous varietals and that all South African grape types are European imports, that didn't preclude creative minds from striving for improvement.

In 1925, Dr. Abraham Perold, the first professor of viticulture at the University of Stellenbosch, developed a cross between Pinot Noir and Cinsault, hoping to combine the nuance and delicacy of the former with the heft and thick-skinned resistance to heat of the latter. The first commercial bottling of Pinotage was released in 1961, and since then it has become an integral part of the South African wine scene. Good Pinotage is filled with wild berry and smoky, gamey notes, a perfect accompaniment to hearty grilled meats and barbeque. So-called "Cape blends" combine Pinotage with a percentage of Cabernet or Syrah or both and can be rich and complex wines. Just as Chenin Blanc is the signature white wine of South Africa, Pinotage is its signature red. Try any of the labels from Fairview, Kanonkop, Simonsig, Spice Route or Clos Malverne for consistently good examples.

And as to those Syrahs and Cabernet Sauvignons, consider yourself in for an unexpected treat. The Syrahs tend to be big and juicy, with plum, blackberry, cocoa and spicy, smoky notes, well made and very approachable. The best of the Cabs are gorgeous, and both varietals are built around a structured core of tannins that brings them into beautiful balance, with good alcohol, focused fruit and excellent acidity. They also display a typical wisp of South African dust that's almost a stamp of origin. Blackberry and cassis, hints of leather, tobacco, fig and coffee, and fine-grained tannins are standard characteristics of the Cabernets. These are wines well worth trying and come from many outstanding wineries, or wine farms, as they're referred to in the Cape regions, among them De Trafford, Fairview, Boekenhoutskloof, Rustenberg, Rust En Vrede, Neil Ellis, LeRiche, Simonsig, Spice Route, Thelema, Finlayson, Warwick, Kanonkop, Ernie Els, Glen Carlou, Meerlust, Flagstone, Rupert and Rothschild. Excellent wines, an exciting region. Try them.

South Africa: Best Beer Bets

Rich and diverse might describe the wine scene on the southern tip of the continent, but the beer market has long been dominated by home-grown SABMiller, now one of the world's largest brewers. Although South African beer-making had the influence of the Europeans who colonized the country—first the Dutch and then the British, not to mention the indigenous beers made for centuries from maize and sorghum—the current offerings are mainly a lackluster array of industrial products.

The most popular are SAB's Castle Lager, Castle Milk Stout, and Black Label, known to locals as Zamalek. It's also getting easier to find Heineken and Amstel and any number of imports in the country, if that's what you've come to South Africa for. Actually, the imports from next-door neighbor Namibia, a stickler for German purity laws, aren't bad either, especially Windhoek Lager.

Not as widely available but a step up are Kulu Draught and the SAB Fransen Street beers. And at least one beer-loving foreign spy claims that a small group of brew pubs, most in the Cape region, are turning out such interesting cups as Mitchell's Raven Stout, Bosun's Best Bitter, Birkenhead Premium Lager, and Tollie's Lager, all of which sound worth a try. And just so you can say you did it, why not latch on to a carton or jug of so-called Zulu beer, one such being Joberg Beer, a traditional sorghum brew, thick, pink, sour and slightly sweet, that's packaged while still fermenting. Holes are punched in the tops of the containers to keep them from bursting, and locals assess the beer's freshness by the foam on the lid. No doubt an acquired taste, but hey, you'll have a great story to tell at your favorite pub back home.

AUSTRALIA

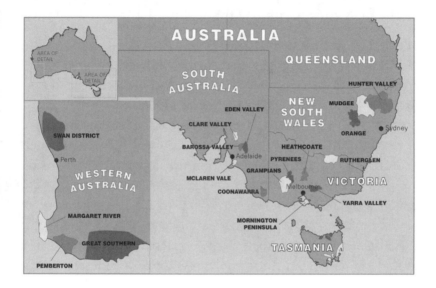

A wine producer of some import, the Land Down Under has had its ups and downs but now seems back on track to achieving consistent quality and innovation. It wasn't too long ago that Australia made its mark on the international wine stage by producing oceans of fruity if somewhat flabby, well-priced, easy-to-drink wines, predominantly Shiraz-based reds and super-ripe Chardonnays, carrying the it-could-be-from-almost-anywhere South Eastern Australia designation. Quaffable? Yes. Distinct? No, and that was the problem. These were wines assembled from juice grown over a huge swath of territory; they were enjoyable if sometimes heavy on the alcohol but devoid of personality and hardly mouthwatering.

Yet even while these simple inexpensive wines were carving out a niche in the "if it's cheap, fruity and not too challenging, I'll drink it" category, Australia's serious winemakers were hard at work behind the scenes. And making some gorgeous wines, though their output was largely ignored by an export market used to Australia as a source of low-cost, critter wines. Fortunately, that's a chapter in the story of Aussie winemaking that's less and less important.

Australia has made a serious commitment to *terroir-* and site-specific wines and to reacquainting the world with its many outstanding offerings. And though they've not had much impact internationally, a diverse group of mainly Italian varieties is also under development. Don't be surprised if you come across Aussie Sangiovese or Aglianico, Nero d'Avola, or even Pinot Gris or Vermentino. I've actually tasted some fairly credible Nebbiolos.

In shape, think of Australia as a bean, its rounded side facing north and its two lobes dipping into the lower latitudes. The outback, the hot desert interior, and the northern tropical regions are generally unsuited for growing wine grapes. But the lobes of this giant bean happen to sit at the same latitude as South Africa and the wine-producing regions of South America. It's here that we find the great *terroirs* responsible for outstanding Rieslings and Shiraz and Sémillon.

Wines to try—Regions to explore:
Let's begin in Sydney, Australia's largest city and capital of the state of New South Wales. This international center of commerce, arts and culture is located on the southeastern coast and is a great place to begin a wine tour of the Land Down Under. Only 80 miles out of town lay the historic Hunter Valley, immensely popular with local wine tourists and a region that produces some of the world's great dry Sémillon.

As a major component of the magnificent Sauternes of Bordeaux, the noble-rot infected Sémillon grape produces what is arguably the greatest sweet wine made. But when it comes to a dry version, nothing rivals Hunter Valley Sémillons. This golden-skinned white, showing rather hard citrus and green apple flavors when young, has the unique capacity to age and improve in the bottle for many years. When fully mature, at ten, fifteen or twenty years, it turns a rich golden yellow with complex honey and burnt toast characteristics most delectable in a white wine.

Nearby are the lesser regions of Orange and Mudgee—lesser in history and notoriety but equal partners with Hunter Valley in terms of producing very good Chardonnay and even better Shiraz, which, like their Sémillon stablemate, can be a touch hard and angular when young but which round out nicely with a few years of bottle age.

Swooping south and then west, "around the corner" so to speak, we come to the state of Victoria, an absolute playground of *terroirs* and gorgeous wines of all sorts. With the city of Melbourne as its epicenter, Victoria's wine regions—in Australia called *GIs*, for *geographic indications*—fan out from sea to mountains and back again. This is a land of slopes and hillsides facing north and south, valleys both wide and narrow, and climates, depending on location, elevation and distance from the sea, that can be either maritime or continental. Overall, however, Victoria has a cool climate, so its white wines tend to the crisp and racy, while its reds are usually medium-bodied, with great acidity, low alcohol and good tannic structure.

There's a practically unending supply of delicious juice in this amalgam of regions, but if I had to pick just one GI, it would be Yarra Valley, with its long-lived, flavorful Pinot Noirs and its peppery, raspberry- and black cherry-flavored, silky-textured Shiraz. Or perhaps Mornington Peninsula, with those fabulous delicate Chardonnays showing fig and melon and white peach. Or maybe I'd choose Nagambie Lakes and its iconic Marsanne, all juicy

138

fruit and honeysuckle when young, not to mention its extraordinary old-vines Cabernet. Or wait, how about Heathcoate, source of so many stunning, densely flavored and deeply colored, glass-coating bottlings of Shiraz, or Rutherglen, home to Australia's most outrageous fortified wines, those crazy tawnies and unctuous, raisiny Muscats and hard-to-get-your-tongue-around sweet and delicious topaques (and please don't ask who came up with that moniker).

And that's just the half of it. This state alone would be worth the trip down under. Just for the wine. Forget the great people and the breathtaking scenery and the ... well, you get the point. Not to mention that just 150 miles offshore lies the island of Tasmania, an increasingly reliable source of complex, serious Pinot Noir and much of Australia's best sparkling wine and sparkling-wine grapes.

Victoria's next-door neighbor is South Australia, source of about half of all wine produced in the country. Most of its wine regions are fairly close to the state capital and largest city, Adelaide, which puts them north of much of Victoria and therefore, aside from elevation-based exceptions, in a generally warmer climate. One could do worse than rent a car and spend a week, or a month, visiting the places near and dear to every Aussie wine lover's heart.

A great start would be to drive 90 minutes north from Adelaide to Clare Valley, source of much of Australia's finest Riesling. And what wonderful Riesling it is! Bone-dry, taut, full-flavored and minerally. World class by any standard. There's even a Riesling Trail to help you get from one great producer to the next. And take a sip of any of the valley's deep, rounded and concentrated Shiraz or Cabernet Sauvignons, frequently blended together and at times including Malbec.

■ *TECHNICAL DRIVEL* ■

We've already explored the importance of acidity in wine, how it gives life and juiciness to wine and helps cleanse and refresh the palate. In a warm climate, it's more difficult to maintain a grape's natural acidity as the heat boosts the ripening and development of sugars while simultaneously reducing the level of acid.

This is nature's way: a fully ripened fruit is sweet and attracts the birds and insects that will spread its seeds, first with the fruit's color and then with its taste. Hard, green, unripe grapes contain seeds that aren't mature, so the plant doesn't "want" them distributed. High levels of acid and bitterness ensure that animals will find the fruit unappealing and leave it to ripen.

In fact, picking grapes at the point where sugars are high but acid levels haven't yet dropped too much is one of the keys to a successful harvest. In many cases, though, this isn't so easily achieved. Sugar levels may be close to optimal, with acids just starting their late-season drop before the grape is fully mature. If picked at this point, the grape skins may be too light in color and the tannins green and hard in the unripe pips (seeds), resulting in a pale wine with harsh, unpleasant tannins.

Some growers leave these grapes to reach full maturity even though sugar levels continue to rise, along with the subsequent alcohol levels of the final wine. One "fix" for this problem is artificial acidification of the grape must while it's fermenting. Another approach, sanctioned in some countries or regions and not in others, is to pick while acid levels are still good and then to add sugar during fermentation to boost the final alcohol level, a process developed in France called chaptalization. The sugar is all converted to alcohol, so it doesn't sweeten the wine but rather rounds it out and brings it into better balance. Manipulating wine using either of these methods is at best a tricky procedure and can lead to a less-than-perfect product.

Fortunately for the winemakers of Clare Valley and certain other warm spots around the world, higher elevations and/or cool nights preserve acid levels despite warm and sunny daytime conditions. Actually, this large "diurnal" shift, or variation from day to nighttime temperatures, can be close to the ideal microclimate for good-quality grapes. Hot, sunny days hasten the ripening process, while cool nights maintain the desired acid levels, leaving grapes that are well balanced and nearly perfect for fine winemaking.

The other region producing great Aussie Riesling is the Eden Valley, also in South Australia. Cool and windy at its higher end, the valley's Rieslings are crisp and floral, with flavors of lime and citrus. Shiraz is the star at the lower end of the valley. Full-bodied, with plum and dark-cherry and even licorice notes, these are at the same time quite elegant and silky. Perhaps the best known, and most highly regarded, of these is Henschke's Hill of Grace.

Just down the road lies the Barossa Valley, Australia's most famous wine district, home of all those marvelous, powerful, fat, full-bodied, richly fruity, intensely flavored bottlings of Shiraz. The Barossa is more than worth the visit, with small, high-quality wineries standing cheek by jowl with the megabrand producers whose labels are known worldwide. It's also a gorgeous destination region peppered with excellent restaurants and accommodations of all sorts. Kind of like tucking America's top craft brewers in among the big industrial producers of pale ales and lagers and setting them all down in the midst of a stunning natural setting with plenty of great food and lodging. And Barossa is the home, if not the sole sourcing region, of Penfolds' Grange, arguably Australia's most famous wine and, along with the Hill of Grace, among the finest Shiraz produced anywhere. Not to slight any of Barossa's Shiraz producers—this is the holy land of New World Shiraz, and the list of outstanding producers is long and deep.

But should you be there, or be looking for wine from the valley, realize that, much as in the Clare Valley, there is some marvelous Cabernet Sauvignon grown here as well, intensely colored, rich and almost classic in flavor, a bit more restrained than the Shiraz. Grenache also does beautifully in the warm Barossa climate, and the numerous 100-year-old-plus vines produce powerful, juicy, almost spicy-sweet versions of this delicious varietal. It's from the Barossa Valley that we get many of those wonderful GSMs (blends of Grenache, Shiraz, and Mourvèdre—or Mataro, as it's called Down Under), that mimic certain of the great wines of the Southern Rhone.

Heading south and skirting the city of Adelaide, one comes to the Adelaide Hills. This is a cool-climate region and the source of complex, supple Chardonnays and, hands down, some of Australia's best Sauvignon Blanc. These wines are top-notch; in fact, with the blending of locally grown Pinot Noir (another cool-climate lover) to the Chardonnay, some extremely refined and expressive sparkling wines are produced here as well. A bit farther on, 20 miles south of Adelaide proper, McLaren Vale also generates wonderful citrusy, peachy Chardonnay as well as rich, velvety, densely-colored Shiraz, sometimes sporting hints of bitter chocolate and often high in alcohol. Like Barossa, McLaren Vale is known for its full-bodied, full-flavored GSMs.

For what many consider Australia's finest Cabernet Sauvignon, one need look no further than the Limestone Coast of South Australia in general, and the wine region of Coonawarra in particular. The vineyards here are focused on the region's signature red soil, known as *terra rossa*, a unique iron-rich deposit some 9 miles long by a mere half-mile to 1 mile wide. The wines produced here show both red and black fruits, soft but distinct tannins, and a firm, classic elegance. They are age-worthy, luscious Cabernets.

From here the Aussie wine tour heads west, way west, to the edge of the continent in the vast state of Western Australia. Close to the ocean along the southwestern corner of the country are a handful of newer and seemingly insignificant GIs. Producing no more than 5% of Australia's wine, these far-removed regions would be easy to overlook if their wines weren't so good. The huge, sparsely populated Great Southern region turns out some excellent Riesling and Chardonnay and very good Shiraz, peppery with spicy blackberry and plum around a finely wrought core. But it's Margaret River that's made people take notice. Its Chardonnay is so pure and intense, concentrated and complex that many consider it the finest in all the land. And the Sauvignon Blanc bursts with grassy, tropical notes that blend beautifully with the lemony, herbal, weighty Sémillon. Add to this some aromatic Cabernet Sauvignon filled with cassis and hints of violets—almost the equal of Coonawarra's—and the sweetest, richest Merlot Australia has to offer and you have a happy ending to a great wine story.

Australia: Best Beer Bets

Oh my, it could be worth the trip just for the beer! Australians have long had the reputation as hard drinkers, binge drinkers even, with beer being their favored sip. Just be sure you don't come across as a bludger (deadbeat, lazy good-for-nothing) or, worse, a piker (one who doesn't drink, or won't drink to excess), though if you're reading this book that's probably unlikely.

Fair dinkum is a good trait or definition to have applied (meaning genuine, honest, or real), and when ordering, though there may be regional differences, request a pot, a pint or a jug. The best-known national brands are Tooheys and Victoria Bitter,

VB for short. Beyond that, the favored brew will depend on which state you're in.

For instance, in Western Australia the brands Swan and Emu are big; in South Australia it's West End, Southwark, and Coopers; Victoria is fond of Victoria Bitter but also Carlton Draught and Melbourne Bitter; in New South Wales, home of Tooheys, look for Reschs, Hahn, or James Squire. And how could you pass up a XXXX (4exs) from Queensland? Or a Cascade or James Boags in Tasmania?

Aussie beer is predominantly lager (even Victoria Bitters is a lager), often pleasing if somewhat industrial, and meant to be served cold. Guinness and other stouts have a dedicated following, though Fosters is really an export brand with little or no impact on the local beer scene.

There's a growing high-quality craft brew movement in Australia, so between sipping VB's or XXXX ask around and see what you can find in terms of bitter ales, pale ales, porters, wheat beers and true pilsners. Here, as in much of the beer-consuming world, a certain segment of tipplers are tiring of the same old same-old and exploring the big bold world of microbrewing. So drink up, mate, and give a shout for the next round.

NEW ZEALAND

Across the Tasman Sea from Australia is the island nation of New Zealand, small in size but huge in the flavors of its wines. This stunningly beautiful, easy-going country ushered itself into the wine consciousness of sippers everywhere with its eye-opening Sauvignon Blancs. Though wine has been produced here since the mid-1800s, it was only in the 1980s that the outside world took notice of the intense, pungent Sauvignon Blancs coming from the Marlborough region of the South Island. There's a strong case to be made that New Zealand Sauvignon Blancs are the finest anywhere. Crisp, grassy, refreshing, almost startling in purity, these wines paved the way for the country's entire modern wine industry.

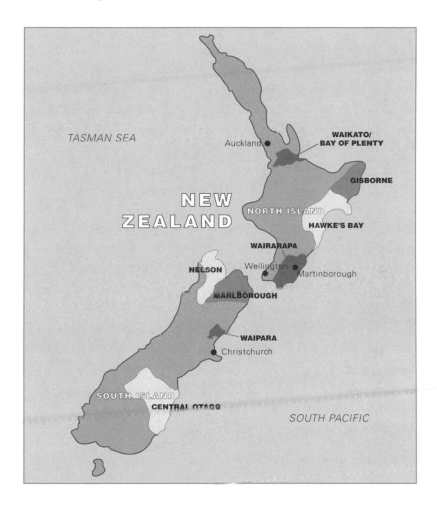

Depending on who's doing the delineating, there are eight, 10, or 15 distinct wine regions split between the North and South Islands. That marvelous Sauvignon Blanc is produced not only in Marlborough but in Hawke's Bay and Wellington, on the North Island, and Nelson, Canterbury and Waipara, on the South Island.

New Zealand is a long, narrow country, a cool-climate region, with most vineyards within a few miles of the sea. Its southern latitude ensures long sunny days, allowing the grapes to ripen fully. As a result, its wines show good acid and structure and rich color. Some quite delicious Chardonnays hail from both islands, from Auckland, Waikato and Bay of Plenty, Gisborne (NZ's preeminent Chardonnay region), Hawke's Bay, Marlborough, and Waipara. The South Island especially delivers with its Rieslings, racy and vibrant and well worth trying, most being slightly off-dry, all citrus and lime and beautifully aromatic.

Excellent Merlot, Cabernet Sauvignon, and Syrah are produced on the North (slightly warmer) Island—most successfully in and around Auckland and Hawke's Bay—though it's really Pinot Noir that has become New Zealand's top red. As the Kiwis get more adept at working with this fickle, thin-skinned variety, they're producing wines that rival the best of either the Old World or the New.

New Zealand Pinot Noir has the elegance of Burgundy, showing pure flavors and fine-grained tannins, and cuts a swath from the dense, plummy, full-bodied Wairarapas and its subregion Martinboroughs (often with a touch of chocolate) to the lighter cherry-flavored versions of Nelson and Marlborough, through the spicy, expressive Waiparas, and on to the intense, structured berry-fruit Pinots of Central Otago. Like New Zealand's Sauvignon Blancs, these are world-class wines, and they just keep getting better.

New Zealand: Best Beer Bets

As in many countries, a few big, so-so lagers dominate the market—think Canterbury Draught, Tui, Steinlager or Speights—generally producing decent, clean, unexciting brews, mostly pale lagers (although Speights puts out a well-regarded Summer Harvest wheat, among other tasty treats).

However, in addition to the various labels owned and controlled by the big boys, and they do have their fans, the Kiwis have a pretty healthy craft brew scene. Most of these new age

146

brewers put out a variety of styles but seem to favor IPAs, ambers and porters. The names to look out for include Epic, Emerson's, Yeastie Boys, Mike's Organic, Renaissance, and Wanaka. And be sure to ask around for the best brew pubs should you be visiting.

ARGENTINA

Standing back to back like long, lanky winemakers, Argentina and Chile form the epicenter of South America's wine scene. Backed up against the north-south spine of the Andes Mountains, Chile claims the west coast and its predominantly Mediterranean climate, gazing out to the sparkling Pacific, while Argentina, in the rain shadow of the Andes and subject to a more continental rain-in-the-winter, hot-days-and-cool-nights climate in the summer, looks east across the pampas to Brazil and Uruguay and ultimately the South Atlantic.

Argentina's wine regions, like Chile's, run the length of the Andes, nestled in high, dry foothills and alluvial plains within sight of the mountains. The industry was built by Italian immigrants and in many sites their Sangiovese, Nebbiolo and Bonarda are still to be found. It's two other varieties, though, that define Argentina's best: Malbec, a red grape originally from Bordeaux, and the aromatic white, Torrontés, whose obscure origins suggest a cross of Muscat of Alexandria and Criolla, brought to the country long ago by Spanish missionaries.

Wines To Try, Regions To Explore

All wine roads (flights, etc.) lead to and through Mendoza, but let's begin in the far-northerly region of Salta. Here it's elevation that beats the heat and lets fine wine grapes grow. Big temperature shifts from day to night keep grape acids at mouthwatering levels while the high UV intensity prods the reds, mainly Cabernet Sauvignon and Malbec, to develop deep colors and fine tannins. But Salta, like nearby La Rioja, is more noted for its fine Torrontés. These medium to light, lovely and crisp whites are highly aromatic, redolent of flowers and tropical fruit, with great acidity and a long finish, and make wonderful food wines.

Skirting the region of San Juan, hot-climate producer of table grapes, vermouth, and brandy, head south, back to the most important Argentinean wine region of Mendoza. In the DO of Luján de Cuyo, just outside the city of Mendoza, and the Uco Valley, high altitude sub-region some fifty miles to the south, the finest Malbecs in the world are produced. Deep, almost electric purple-black in color with aromas of damson fruit and blackberry compote, these gorgeous, full-bodied wines far eclipse the Malbec produced in the varietal's native region of southwestern France. In fact, more Malbec is now grown in Argentina than in any other country.

This is a wine for meat, for the big, burly cuts of grilled or roasted beef and spicy sausages that are such a part of the gaucho and Argentine experience. And while in Mendoza, don't overlook the excellent Tempranillos or Chardonnays, or the exciting Cabernet Sauvignons coming from Maipú, next door to Luján de Cuyo.

On to Patagonia ... or at least close to it. The most southerly regions of Argentina are Rio Negro and Neuquén. As might be imagined, these cool climates have proved best for Torrontés as well as bracing Sauvignon Blancs and Sémillon. And as wine-growers are always experimenting, there are even some plantings of Pinot Noir here.

Argentina: Best Beer Bets

Cerveza Quilmes, a standard, industrial pale lager, is by far the most popular beer in Argentina. It leads a crew of big national brands including Isenbeck, Schneider, Iguana, Andes and Salta. European beers Heineken, Warsteiner, and Stella Artois also figure in the local scene.

Argentines love to socialize, to get together and share food, drink and conversation, so there's no shortage of restaurants or bars, where it's fairly easy to come across Brahma (Brazil), Duvel, Chimay, Grolsch, Guinness and others (Budweiser even). But most exciting are the craft beers and microbrews.

Beer-lover kudos go to Antares (big and getting bigger), Buller Brewing (look for its brew pub in Buenos Aires), Otro Mundo, Barba Roja, Mendoza-based Cerveza Jerome, and El Bolsón. Not all are available throughout the country, so you may have to hunt a little. Most of these brewers make a variety of styles, with stouts, IPAs, amber ales, Scotch ales, doppelbocks and dunkler bocks being especially popular. Also common is the 1-liter bottle, not so you can get a big head on but because these folks do love to sit and sip and share. All in all, not a bad philosophy.

CHILE

On the west slope of the Andes, less than an hour from Mendoza as the condor flies, lies Chile's capital city of Santiago, also the approximate midpoint of its wine regions. Vineyards span a band some 800 miles north to south girdling the center of this long, narrow country. Chile's wine regions are almost a mirror image of those in Argentina: anchored on the ocean side of the cordillera by Santiago and on the eastern side by Mendoza, both run within a hundred miles of the mountains (in Chile because the entire country averages only a hundred miles in width, in Argentina because that's where the best soil and climatic conditions are for growing wine grapes).

For Chile, however, the major determinant of *terroir* is not distance from either the equator to the north or Antarctica to the south but rather where the vineyards lie between the coast and the mountains. Those districts right along the coast are subject to the Humboldt Current, which bathes the vines in a blanket of cool, moist air, while farther inland and higher in elevation, grapes benefit from long sunny days and acid-preserving temperature drops at night.

Wines To Try, Regions To Explore

Chile's most northerly regions, much like Salta and La Rioja east of the Andes in Argentina, should be far too hot for successful viticulture. Here in the Elqui and Limarí valleys, however, it's daytime sea breezes and nighttime fog, instead of altitude, that make it all possible. As might be imagined, some gorgeous cool-weather Sauvignon Blancs and Chardonnays are produced here, along with deeply colored, pure and peppery Syrahs and lush, taut versions of Carmenére.

Skip south to the east-west-running Aconcagua Valley. Known for a warm, dry climate and rocky, well-drained soils, its best wines are red: Cabernet Sauvignon and Merlot in particular, with Carmenére as well. Near the western end of the valley, funneling down to the Pacific, is the relatively new region of

Casablanca. Unlike the warmer interior, the Casablanca Valley is cool and wet and frequently under a layer of coastal fog. And though this damp-and-cool combination creates challenges for the winegrowers, Casablanca is putting out wines that rank among Chile's most exciting Sauvignon Blancs, Chardonnays, and Pinot Noirs, all varieties that reach their peak expression in cooler climes.

Chile's signature grape, Carmenére, is an echo of old Bordeaux. When the phylloxera infestation devastated the vineyards of France, it eliminated the variety known then as Grand Vidure, a mainstay of Bordeaux. Cuttings had been brought from France to Chile in the nineteenth century and were confused with Merlot. Not until the 1990s did DNA testing establish the grape's true identity.

Wines made from Carmenére are deep crimson in color and show cherry-like red fruit and an herbaceous character, with spicy, sometimes smoky and chocolaty notes. Carmenére tends to have soft, easy tannins and, though used mainly for blending, can be quite dramatic as a stand-alone variety when handled with care.

Moving to the Central Valley, on the doorstep of Santiago and directly across the mountains from the city of Mendoza, is the district of Maipo. Originally planted in the 19th century by wealthy families from Santiago with vines imported from Bordeaux, this region made Chile famous with its lush and supple Cabernet Sauvignons, intense with black-currant fruit and hints of eucalyptus. This region is close to the capital, convenient for the traveler and home to many outstanding wineries.

Farther south is Rapel Valley, whose highly praised sub-districts of Colchagua and Cachapoal have proved to be fabulous terrain for both Cabernet Sauvignon and Merlot, with Syrah, Sauvignon Blanc and Carmenére running a close second. This is an easy 110-mile run outside Santiago. These Chilean districts are all amazing, filled with history, landscapes and architecture that make every turn of the corner an adventure. Great vineyards in an exciting, exotic locale can be a compelling reason to travel the wine world.

Especially when the next stop is the Curicó Valley. Workhorse of Chilean wine production, with significantly more winter rainfall than Rapel or Maipo, this region produces consistently good and honestly priced Cabernet Sauvignon and Sauvignon Blanc. Continuing "down" the length of Chile is that champion district of terrific Carmenére, the Maule Valley. (You'll note that many Chilean wine districts are valleys. This is because the foothills and mountain valleys of the Andes mountains, so close to the coast along the entire length of Chile, run east to west, from peaks down to the sea. Grapes grown farther east, or upland, take on more long-sunny-day and high altitude characteristics than the same varieties from vineyards closer to the ocean.)

From Maule, at about the same latitude as the southernmost extremes of the greater Mendoza region, the wine trail skips to the Bio-Bio Valley. This cool-climate region centered on the town of Los Angeles seems to have a great future, evolving from the production of brandy grapes to a beautiful offering of aromatic white wines, including Riesling, Viognier, and Gewurztraminer. The days of green Chilean reds and unexciting whites are over. Chile and its winemakers have moved strongly forward; they're now making tremendous wines from north to south.

Chile: Best Beer Bets

Cristal beer, a dependably flavorless, pale lager, is Chile's top brand, and Escudo—nicely bitter, somewhat hoppy, yellow-gold in color—is second. They account for the bulk of local beer sales. The German, southern part of the country produces Kunstmann, which has a good dark bock, a lovely pale ale and a delicious lager, all brewed according to sixteenth century German beer laws. But it's the *cervezas artesanals*, or artisan beers, that provide the best bang for the buck in this country.

One such is the Szot Microbrewery in Santiago, founded by a U.S. expat and his Chilean wife. They brew an award-winning lineup that includes a hoppy, bitter pale ale, a richer, malty amber ale, and the excellent Negra Stout. Another notable brewery is Cervezera del Puerto in Valparaiso, also putting out a pale ale, an amber ale and something between a stout and a porter called Barba Negra.

These and most of Chile's *artesanals* are for the most part small-batch, handcrafted beers. Some might be a bit too sweet, others overly alcoholic, but the craft beer and microbrewing scene is quite new and still finding its footing. Chileans are fun, open people, so ask around for local breweries and stop in to the local pubs. Santiago (abutting the Maipo Valley wine district), Valparaiso (just down the road from Casablanca Valley), and Concepcion (Bio-Bio, here we come) all have vibrant small breweries and enthusiastic brewers.

A Quick Note

That covers the major wine centers of the Old World and the New. The list isn't complete, nor is it meant to be. But it gives you what you need to navigate 98% of what you're likely to encounter, be it on the shelves of your local wine retailer, on the ground visiting the world's great wine regions, or just chatting it up with your boss or new best friends about wine in general.

The beers mentioned may or may not be available in this country, but they are most certainly part of the landscape in their homelands. So take a trip, broaden your horizons, sip some wine and suck some suds. Enjoy. Life is good.

Oh yeah, we have one more country to cover ...

UNITED STATES

Back to the good old US of A, where in every one of the fifty states, for one reason or another, wine is made. In the regions to be covered, i.e. California, Oregon, and Washington state, much of that wine is world class, and often the envy of winemakers worldwide.

Some good wine also comes from New York (very good, actually), Virginia, Texas, Colorado, Missouri, Ohio, Illinois, even Michigan and Massachusetts. Should you be spending time in any of these states, it makes for an enjoyable day to tour the wineries and taste what they're putting in the bottle. You may find a mixture of good and not so good, but it's fun to try them all, and a great way to learn.

In most other states the majority of wineries either produce fruit wines or truck grapes halfway across the country to make second-rate versions of first-rate varietals or rent themselves out as "bucolic" wedding venues. Not that there's anything wrong with blueberry wine or having a wedding under the rose arbor next to the vines; it's just that fruit wines, while fun and easy, don't fall within the purview of fine wines, and wineries that pay more attention to parties and celebrations than to building the quality of their wines are really in a different business.

Old World winemaking is based on techniques and traditions that have evolved over hundreds of years, intended to maximize the quality of wine produced vis-à-vis its *terroir* and to guarantee that consumers (especially the shippers and merchants on whom the reputation of wine regions depended) were getting the "real" thing. The New World is little influenced by tradition and more focused on obtaining a quality product by any means, often through innovation and experimentation.

While the former approach may generate greater consistency, the latter, despite its fits and starts, can and, in regards to wine-making, has raised the bar for everyone. Be it the use of stainless steel tanks, greater emphasis on cleanliness in the winery, or improvements to viticulture that result in superior grapes, the New World has pushed the envelope. And while hardly exclusive to the United States, this country's wine community has certainly been a major factor in winemaking and the development of wine styles worldwide.

Wines To Try, Regions To Explore: California

Let's start with the eight-hundred-pound gorilla in the room: California. This state produces 90% of all wine made in the U.S. and has garnered a spot among the globe's top winemaking regions. Much of that has to do with weather—generally one tremendous vintage after another—and with a lush, fruit-driven style that's much more in-your-face than the restrained balance of fruit, fermentation, and aging characteristics typical of Old World wines.

A good example can be found in the Pinot Noirs of the Santa Rita Hills, a small, well-regarded appellation outside Santa Barbara in southern California. While the region might seem too warm for Pinot Noir, this small range of hills only a dozen miles from the Pacific is cooled almost constantly, either by sea breezes or by fog. The resulting fruit produces lush, full-bodied wines with lovely Pinot notes of spice and tea and a variety of red berry fruit. Not very Burgundian, too dark and too full and too alcoholic to be French Pinot Noir, but exceptionally good and very Pinot-like anyway. Much the same comparison can be made with the state's Chardonnays and Cabernet Sauvignons as well. And by the way, if you've come this far, don't miss a side trip to Los Olivos, a tiny town just a few miles away whose main street has become home to a very large handful of casual but excellent tasting rooms.

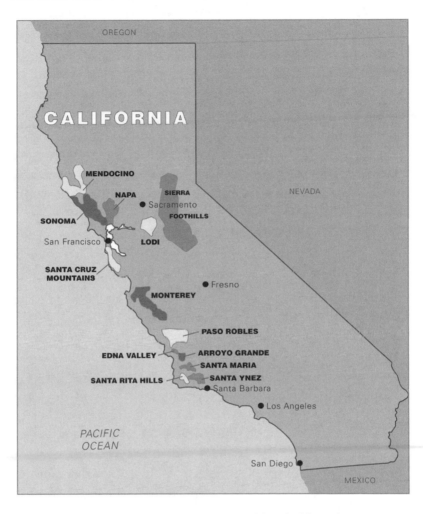

Next up would have to be Paso Robles, halfway between Los Angeles and San Francisco and heart of the Central Coast AVA (American Viticultural Area). Centered on the town of the same name, Paso Robles is a gorgeous area of steep rolling hills and a variety of soil types. Home base of the so-called Rhone Rangers, the wineries in this fast-growing area produce terrific Syrah, Grenache, and Mourvèdre, often blended together, in addition to wonderful Zinfandel, Cabernet Sauvignon, Petite Sirah and Chardonnay. This is one of California's hotter regions, the cool ocean breezes blocked for the most part by the Santa Lucia Mountains. Alcohol levels tend to be high and the wines are rich, powerful and full-bodied.

Closer to San Francisco, from the north side of Monterrey Bay to the Silicon Valley towns of San Jose, Sunnyvale and Mountain View, take a drive through the Santa Cruz Mountains AVA, a small region studded with some of California's most notable wineries and iconic winemakers. Breathtaking vistas and winding roads lead quickly from population centers to surprisingly rural settings for vineyards famed for their Zinfandel, Pinot Noir, and Chardonnay. And when in San Francisco, set aside some time to hop aboard the Oakland/Alameda Ferry, take a quick sail across the bay, and visit Rosenblum Cellars. There just aren't many high-quality urban wineries, and Rosenblum, a well-known Zinfandel producer, occupies a unique site at the very edge of San Francisco Bay.

From the spectacular City by the Bay, it's only about ninety minutes north across the Golden Gate Bridge to Napa Valley. After passing through the cool-climate southern end of both the Napa and Sonoma valleys—i.e., Los Carneros—beneficiary of chilly fog banks and cooling breezes off San Pablo Bay that make for crisp, taut Chardonnays and zesty Pinot Noirs, you'll land in downtown Napa, ground zero of American wine culture. One immediately notices a) the traffic (more than 4 million wine lovers visit Napa Valley every year), b) the topography, which allows for fifteen smaller AVAs within Napa (be sure to visit Stag's Leap, a benchland along the eastern side of the valley; Howell Mountain, a few miles to the north; Oakville, Rutherford and St. Helena, in the mid-valley; and Mt. Veeder and the Diamond Mountain districts, on the west), and c) the money (Napa land is mucho pricey, and most of the wineries and tasting rooms are deluxe operations).

Though the wines here are expensive, very good Napa Valley Cabs, Merlots and Chardonnays are very good indeed. In fact, it was the triumph of a 1973 Stag's Leap Wine Cellars Cabernet Sauvignon and a 1973 Chateau Montelena Napa Valley Chardonnay at the famed Paris Tasting of 1976 that kick-started this region's rapid and deserved rise to the top of the wine world. And this from a region less than one-eighth the size of Bordeaux.

From the town of Napa, head south and then west on Route 12 around the southern end of the Mayacamas Mountains into Sonoma. This is a charming old mission town at the southern end of the Sonoma County AVA. It's immediately apparent that you've left the "rural congestion" of Napa Valley and arrived in a more laid-back outpost of winemaking. Sonoma is stretched out, over twice the size of Napa, and borders the ocean. Sub-regions that shouldn't be missed as you wend your way north include Glen Ellen, Russian River (outstanding Pinot Noir thanks to that lovely ocean influence) and the Dry Creek and Alexander Valley AVAs outside Healdsburg. Expect to find some excellent Cabernet Sauvignons, Sauvignon Blancs and Zinfandels from a list of wineries that reads like a who's who of top wine producers.

**Chile has its Carmenére, Argentina its Malbec, but in California the home-grown variety of note is Zinfandel. This all-American grape that makes rich, spicy, peppery, brambly, berry-fruited, high-alcohol all-American deliciousness actually hails from Croatia.
The original family name was *Crljenak Kaštelanski*, and Italian Primitivo is the sibling Zinfandel never knew it had. But not to worry—it has been lovingly adopted and nurtured by the winegrowers of California for well over a hundred years.**

159

> Because Zinfandel ripens irregularly—there are usually very green, immature berries in the same bunch with dark-colored, fully ripe ones—the variety does best in hot climates with long hang times.
> Of course, getting all the grapes ripe requires many of them to reach quite high sugar levels, hence the typically high alcohol levels of 15% and even 16%. While Zins can and are made in a more elegant style, this is unfortunately not the current trend.

Lake and Mendocino counties are next up, to the north, producing luscious, deeply-colored Petite Sirahs, bold Zinfandels and, along the Mendocino coast, some cult Pinot Noirs. This is low-key wine country, nothing fancy, just good, real, and immensely enjoyable. Moving inland toward Sacramento for all you budding politicians, brings one to Lodi, about 40 minutes south of the capital, and the Sierra Foothills some 45 minutes east. Both these down-home wine regions feature numerous 100-year-old-plus Zinfandel vines and produce rich, full-bodied Cabernet Sauvignons, Syrahs and luscious, fat Chardonnays. The folks here are wonderful, the wineries welcoming and the vibe very cool and kind of craft brewery-ish.

Wines To Try, Regions To Explore: Oregon

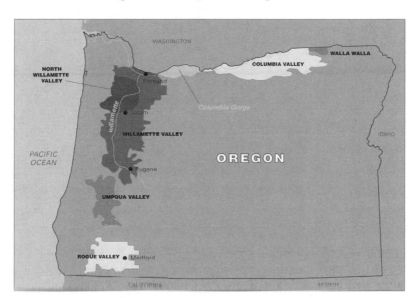

Oregon is home to the diverse, eclectic Southern Oregon AVA, which includes the Rogue and Umpqua valleys, but the state is internationally renowned for its Willamette Valley AVA, some 150 miles long and 50 miles wide and the center of production for what may be the finest, most Burgundian Pinot Noirs of the New World. The heart of this region, the North Willamette Valley, is a mere 45-minute drive south and a bit west of Portland, nestled between the low-rise Coastal Range to the west and the Cascades to the east, and extends as far south as Salem. Winters here are cool and wet, summers hot and dry. And the wine is outstanding year round.

This is a beautiful landscape of open, rolling hills, a relaxed, easy-going region where tasters are welcome and it's not unusual for the sky to be filled with rainbows. In addition to the Willamette's magnificent Pinot Noirs, look for exceptional Chardonnays and Pinot Gris.

Wines To Try, Regions To Explore: Washington

There may be no more exciting region in all of USA winedom than Washington state. It's a region surprisingly little known yet one that produces a plethora of extraordinarily good, even great wine. A lush, wet rain forest of a coastline, snowy Mount Rainier, the Space Needle, Seattle and its Pike Place Market, Puget Sound, salmon and Dungeness crab are the landmarks and images that represent Washington to most people. Hardly the environment for outstanding vineyards. And in fact, it's not.

But just over the mountains, in the hot, dry desert of eastern Washington, the combination of silty, windblown, easily drained soil, cold winters and hot summers, clear skies and long hours of daylight make for almost ideal grape-growing conditions. The resulting fruit is deeply colored, free from pests or mildew, with a close-to-perfect balance of sugar, acid, and tannin. Much of it is trucked back to the coastal region surrounding Seattle, where many of Washington's wineries have chosen to locate.

The first stop for any wine lover should be the town of Woodinville, about a half-hour north of Seattle, where some of the state's signature wineries, from largest to smallest, either have wineries or tasting rooms open to the public. This little burg is the perfect option for anyone with only a day or two in Seattle, as it's possible to taste a wide-ranging, representative sample of what's being produced throughout the state. Of course, for the best Washington wine experience, head east across the Cascades and point yourself first to Yakima, home to some of the state's top Syrah, Merlot, and Cabernet Sauvignon vineyards, noted in particular for the elegance and complexity of their fruit, and then to Benton City and the nearby Red Mountain AVA. The wineries here are worth an entire day. Red Mountain wines are big, lush and powerful. Just down the road is the Tri-Cities region of Richland, Pasco, and Kennewick, at the heart of the huge

Columbia Valley wine region. You'll find wineries to the left of you and wineries to the right.

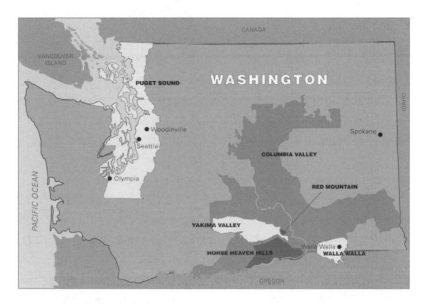

By now you'll realize that Washington's Merlots are richer, deeper and more serious than almost any you've had outside the Right Bank of Bordeaux, that the Syrahs are peppery and gamey and juicy, and that Washington vintners love to blend: Cabernet, Merlot and Cabernet Franc, or Cabernet and Syrah, or Sémillon and Sauvignon Blanc. The Chardonnays are crisp, yet full-bodied, the Rieslings retain just enough sweetness to balance their acidity, and the Viogniers are a bit fruitier while showing more restraint in the perfume department than their French cousins.

But don't stop before you reach Walla Walla, home to another cornucopia of outstanding wineries. This is a town that celebrates its wine culture, and you could do worse than to check into a local hotel or B&B for a long weekend. Wend your way through the many boutique wineries surrounding the local airport or the cluster of exceptionally good producers south of town.

Washington is a place where *terroir* really counts, and since wineries often use grapes from various locales, look for vineyard and AVA designations on the labels, among them Boushey, Ciel du Cheval, Champoux, Stoneridge, Pepper Bridge, Horse Heaven Hills, Wahluke Slope and Rattlesnake Hills.

United States: Best Beer Bets

There's no shortage of beer in the U.S., although, as in many countries, much of it is mass-produced industrial lager, with neither pizzazz nor personality. Fortunately, the United States also happens to be among the leaders of the worldwide craft beer movement; delicious suds are to be found from sea to shining sea. There are said to be in the neighborhood of 2,000 craft brewers nationwide, roughly split between brewpubs and craft or microbreweries, which makes for lots of great drinking.

Of course, no one can visit that many pubs or one-shot micros, but we're still left with the hundreds of outstanding, more widely distributed craft brews, from the largest, the Boston Beer Company, maker of the very good to excellent Sam Adams line—actually a craft brewer so good, so innovative and so successful that many purists now claim it's too big to be deemed worthy of the *craft beer* moniker—to the smallest of the small, whoever that may be, poured in two unaffiliated pubs and available, possibly, in one or two local stores.

There are however, a string of loci that road-tripping beer hounds should be aware of. California, which claims more than 200 breweries, leads the pack in sheer numbers. It's home to such venerable beer-makers as Sierra Nevada, Anchor Brewing, Stone Brewing Co. and Lagunitas. The Pacific Northwest is another center of good taste; just note Pyramid Breweries and Mac and Jack's in the Seattle area and Oregon's heavyweight lineup, composed in part of Full Sail, Rogue Ales, and Deschutes Brewery.

Colorado is also a serious player. Many of its best are strung along the Front Range from Fort Collins south and include New

Belgium Brewing, Flying Dog Brewery, Avery Brewing and the Boulder Beer Company. In the Midwest, Chicago gives us, among others, Goose Island Brewery and Revolution Brewing, whose brewpub grub is over the top, Michigan claims Bell's Brewery and Indiana is home to Three Floyds. Hopping to New England, in addition to the Boston Beer Company, we find some 130 other breweries, including the deservedly acclaimed craft brew pioneer Harpoon Brewery, also in Boston; Shipyard and Allagash, both in Maine; and such notables as Magic Hat in Vermont, and Redhook Ale and Smuttynose Brewing of New Hampshire.

Yet this list barely scratches the surface. How can you not mention Victory Brewing in Pennsylvania, Boulevard Brewing in Kansas City, Brooklyn Brewery in New York, or (please kneel) Dogfish Head in tiny Delaware? And don't despair if you're off the beaten path. Ever heard of Hoppin' Frog in Akron or La Cumbre Brewing in Albuquerque? Well, you probably will, and soon; they're new, they know their stuff and they're winning awards.

And the names! If beer dulls the senses, these craft brewers haven't heard about it. Witness this list of individual beers and ales for a sampling of wit and creativity: Old Crustacean, Gumball Head, Fear and Trembling, Pier Rat Porter, Neighbor of the Beast, Ruination, Brewtus Maximus, Chet's Nuts, Night-Rider Nitro, Commercial Suicide, Daddy's Little Helper, Face Down Brown, Altar Boy, Farmer's Daughter, Blushing Monk (I should say), My Bloody Valentine, Pliny the Elder, Life and Limb. To say nothing of the hundreds of styles, from IPAs to amber ales to brown ales to stouts and porters, to barley wines and wee heavies, from pilsners to lagers, and dunkels and bocks, dubbels and tripels and witbiers and saisons, and lest we forget, lambics and pumpkins and smoked beer and chili beer—yes, even chili beer. Whew! And hyper beer—if you like a brew at 20% alcohol that'll knock you on your keister after just one. Talk about a short session.

Now that you've had a quick tour around the world of wine (with more than a handful of great beers thrown in for good measure), make it a point to try all the styles and varieties you can. Be it red, white, rosé or sparkling each has its place, and much to offer the savvy aficionado. If you're able to travel and visit the regions discussed, you can be sure of a new level of richness and interest in your overall experience. If not, enjoy a taste of the world via the shelves of your local wine store. And as you sip, remember that someone, at some time in the past, on beautiful hillsides or steep rocky slopes, pruned the vines and picked the grapes and created that wonderful beverage now in your glass.

■ ■ ■ ■

11

Finding Your Own Inimitable Style: How To Drink Wine, Buy Wine & Boost Your Coolness Quotient

Assuming you've sipped through some portion of the recommended wines, you have, no doubt, discovered that certain of them appeal to you more than others. No one likes everything, nor should they. Our palates are as individual as our personalities. You may have found Bordeaux bewildering, Rieslings too racy, Syrahs simply not to your taste. Yet Burgundies beguile, Cavas caress, and Zinfandel make you zmile. As they say, there's no accounting for taste. And there's no need to excuse your preferences.

In fact, a tried and true approach to working your way into the wine world is to openly declare your preferences, especially if there's some reasoning or an interesting anecdote or two in support. The reality is that wine people appreciate an independent thinker as long as he or she is more than a strident dullard promoting a singular perspective.

In other words, if you bring, order, or show up with a bottle of Côt (Malbec) from Cahors (a minor region of France) and just explain that you prefer the Old World qualities of it, the leather and tannins and minerality, to the lush fruity, juiciness of Argentine Malbecs, you will be accorded a measure of respect. You may get no agreement, though everyone will be anxious to try what you've brought, but you'll definitely be welcome in the group.

Or should you profess an affection for Barbaresco because it's a bit more approachable than a traditional Barolo, or for a Santorini Assyrtiko because the thought of its origin in ancient Greece, among the waters known to and sailed upon by Odysseus, intrigues you, you're on the right path.

A tidbit of knowledge—whether regarding the tannic Old World character of Côt relative to the inky juiciness of Argentinean Malbec, the openness and approachability of Barbaresco versus Barolo (though in truth, tasted blind and side by side, most wine geeks couldn't tell the difference anyway), or the classical allusions of wines from the Greek islands—may be the sole morsel of wine esoterica in your eno-toolbox, but if it's interesting and true, it's still interesting and true. And it will have currency with wine people. As you absorb other such nuggets, add them to your arsenal. This is how any knowledge base is built. With time, you'll gain a broader picture of the wine world in general and of your own likes and dislikes, with stories and anecdotes to back them up.

EDUCATING YOUR PALATE

The only caveat—and it's an important one—is to try high-quality wines. A second-rate Merlot or Chenin Blanc is second rate and seldom conveys the true measure of a variety. Don't be drawn to the cheapest bottle in the store. Look instead for one more highly recommended, and most likely more expensive, though it needn't be by much. This doesn't mean drink yourself to penury; it means inform your palate with high-quality wines. Low-cost wines are not the product of top-notch fruit; typically they make use of younger grapes or those from a less desirable vineyard site or from a "commercial" winery more concerned with quantity than quality. Only by tasting the *good* stuff will you experience the typicity, the classic nuances and characteristics of a variety, allowing you the opportunity to honestly and accurately assess your preferences.

All of which directs you to the wines you most enjoy, the ones you'll want to have at home. (Of course, this should never stop you from trying unfamiliar wines or varietals. True enthusiasts always have a selection of oddball bottles they've picked up simply out of curiosity.)

But with these other now-familiar new favorites in your life, it's quite easy to inquire of your main squeeze, "Baby, would you like a glass of so-and-so? It comes from a little vineyard in Lodi, about an hour from Lake Tahoe."

Wow. Not bad. Nice start to a promising evening.

Or say a couple of brew buddies show up. "Hey, dudes, lemme turn your suds-soaked palates on to something really good," you say. Squints and cocked heads, a few mumbles re: the new big shot. "Just try this." You pour everyone a glass of something terrific that you'd never heard of three months before. "Tell me that's not intensely delicious."

Raised eyebrows and nods of agreement from the brew crew now. Coolness quotient definitely on the rise.

Project yourself into similar scenes of enjoyment and sharing—with the in-laws, your siblings, that hot neighbor down the hall, even your boss! Don't pretend to know what you don't; in fact, if asked about something relating to wine that you don't know, just admit it. But don't hold back on what you do know, either. If you love a certain wine, say so; if you've heard or read an unusual tidbit about a particular region or winery, share it; let people know that you're learning about wine, that you really enjoy it. Interest, exploration, and passion—all very cool.

WINE SHOPPING

Of course, you will also start frequenting the aisles of a (hopefully) good wine shop/liquor store, maybe the same place where you already pick up your beer. Typical store layouts arrange wine either by country or by varietal. A few try categorizing by general style—e.g., light and fruity or rich and full-bodied—which might be helpful for someone who's never bought a bottle of wine or knows nothing about the subject, but that's a category you're no longer part of.

Even the "by varietal" approach has serious drawbacks. Where do you find blends, for example, or unusual varieties the store has only one or two bottlings of? Or how do you find a Bordeaux Superieur in a long line of alphabetized Merlots or an even longer row of Cabernet Sauvignons if you don't have a specific producer or chateau name?

So, in most cases it's "by country," which makes sense because that's how most people learn about wine: by country and by region. In any case, feel free to wander the aisles, to get a sense of the breadth and depth of the wines available. If something looks interesting, pick it up and read the labels, front and back. Some will tell you next to nothing, others are a mini-education in the wine you're holding.

You'll quickly discover which stores carry the wines or wine styles you prefer and which are most reasonable as far as price is concerned. Some wine shops just have a better vibe than others. Maybe it's the shelving or the selection or the overall atmosphere created by the folks who work there.

And when you get the inevitable "Can I help you find something?" go for it. Give the clerk a chance to be a valuable resource. Certainly not all wine merchants will be, but the good ones are worth knowing and utilizing. Some know far less than you do; others have studied wine with passion for years and can be of tremendous help. After all, there's nothing wrong with saying to your friends or family, "My wine guy down at such-and-such a store pointed me to this outstanding Naoussa. What do you say we try it with these lamb burgers?" Kind of impressive, actually.

As a beer buyer, you know that most domestic brews carry a "best by" or "consume by" date on their labels to save you from going home with a funky monkey in your bag. Theoretically, the higher the alcoholic strength and the more hops in a beer, the longer they should maintain their freshness. But that lovely hoppiness that attracted you to a particular brew in the first place fades with time; quality-conscious brewers want you to drink those hop monsters now, today, as soon as possible, while the volatile hop aromas are still at full strength. Despite their history of long distance travel (high alcohol and heavily hopped to prevent spoilage on long sea voyages from Britain to India) today's IPAs are best enjoyed sooner rather than later. On the flip side of this barley-minted coin, doppelbocks, Imperial stouts, sour ales, and Belgian strong ales (alcohol levels of 6% to 7% and higher) can easily deal with a year or two of cool, climate-controlled aging.

Imports do have their own challenges, though. It's a long way from a foreign brewery to your local retailer, with multiple stops and much transferring of cargo along the way—an arduous journey that may or may not see your highly anticipated Scotch ale or Munich dunkel properly handled (i.e., in a temperature-controlled container during transport, a climate-controlled warehouse to keep it in good shape once it reaches local shores, and a refrigerated truck for final delivery to your favorite bottle shop—the same regimen of care you hope was observed when shipping the imported wines you buy). Otherwise, the best approach is to shop at a clean, well-maintained store that moves a lot of product.

Never buy a lonely six-pack that's been on the shelf so long it's coated in dust. And should you get a bad or spoiled beer—or bottle of wine—from anywhere, return it and request your money back (again, unless you live in an area where refunding opened bottles is legally prohibited). No reputable operation would refuse to stand behind its inventory. Of course, all bets are off if your beer comes home in a growler, in which case you need to drain that sucker within a couple of days for max freshness and enjoyment.

But when it comes to wine shopping "best by" dates aren't part of the equation. In fact, that lonely old, dust-covered bottle may be exactly what you *are* looking for. (An exception is any light-bodied, unoaked white wine, most of which are best consumed within a year or two of vintage. Avoid that six year old Pinot Grigio in the sale bin. Its best days have long ago come and gone.)

Critical elements in a wine shop are sun, temperature and position of the bottles. If you stroll into a shop and see the afternoon sun beating down on the end rack of wine, you may as well assume those bottles are ruined. Heat is not wine's friend, which is the reason that good wine shops keep the thermostat down. A cool shop says someone knows what they're doing and cares about the condition of their product. Position is also important; wine bottles, whenever possible, should be stored on their sides. This keeps the wine in contact with the cork and prevents the cork from drying out and letting air leak into the bottle. In a store with rapid turnover of inventory this may be less crucial, but a ten year old bottle of Barolo standing upright in dry air on a top shelf should give you pause.

TASTING GROUPS

Beyond shopping and enjoying your spoils with a few close friends, you might want to join, or start, a wine-tasting group. This can be completely informal, just a few fellow wine lovers who share an interest in increasing their knowledge of the grape. Everyone brings a bottle, maybe of the same variety but from different regions or vintages or producers, to contrast, compare and rank. Or maybe different varieties but from the same country.

Or have someone provide a particular food and the others in the group all have to bring a wine to match.

There's no limit as to what can be done. All the way up to very formal tastings where no food is allowed (all those lovely food aromas make it difficult to assess the wine), where perfume and aftershave is unequivocally unwelcome, for the same reason, where scores are kept and compared, dissected and discussed, and where the tasting is usually blind (and the attitudes sometimes follow).

But however you do it, make sure it's a good time. A tasting for beer-drinking friends is likely to be quite different from one for your new wine geeks-in-arms. Try holding a few tastings of different kinds and see which *you* enjoy the most. Get your beer drinking friends involved in some wine tasting and your wine drinking friends into beer tasting. There's no right or wrong, no absolutes. If you want to get the girlfriends or the guys together for a summertime tasting of fifteen rosés, do it.

One final tip regarding tastings and wine get-togethers: it almost always makes sense to invite a true knowledgeable, experienced wine drinker (one without the overbearing wine "guru" personality) to such events. These types can answer many of the questions your other guests might have, you'll probably learn a thing or two from observing and talking with them, and best of all, they like to bring great wine to these soirees. Indeed, they frequently pull hard-to-find gems from their own cellars to share with whoever's present. Real wine people are generous. Spend some time with them and it's practically guaranteed you'll have the opportunity to taste wines you could otherwise never find or afford. True wine lovers take great pleasure in sharing the best of what they have.

■ ■ ■ ■

12

The Secrets of Food & Wine Pairing: How To Eat, Drink & Be Merry Every Time

The topic of food-and-wine pairing is seriously overdone. You'd think it was advanced rocket science to hear some of the self-proclaimed experts prattle on about "the perfect match" or "the ideal pairing."

Sure, tannins seem harsher with spicy foods, more acidic wines cut cream sauces nicely, matching peppery or fruity or earthy dishes with a peppery Syrah or a fruity Dolcetto or an earthy Pinot Noir usually makes for a good match, but so what? How about a fruity Grenache with that pepper steak or a peppery Zweigelt with that rather bland but quite tasty Wiener Schnitzel—pairings that ignore the rules but that are every bit as good. The secret is … that there are no secrets, only a few common sense caveats. Just drink what you like and enjoy your food.

Don't forget, the purpose is to enhance *your* experience, not to follow a set of arbitrary dictates that someone else, with too much time on his or her hands, has declared to be the one or the only or the best way to choose what you should drink with dinner.

And never drink something you don't like because a magazine article or wine column has declared it a perfect match with whatever you're eating. If you don't like a wine—because it's red and very tannic or white and over-oaked or sweet or sour or whatever—it makes for a decidedly *imperfect* match. So begin with something you enjoy. Whether you're having it with food or not. Just using your common sense will assure that you have a pretty decent food-and-wine match about nine times out of ten.

The general guidelines say pair a rich, heavy food dish with a rich, full-bodied wine. Heavy food with a full-bodied wine; rich flavor with rich flavor. Hmm ... okay. Or match something light, say oysters or white fish, with an equally light and delicate wine. Sounds reasonable, but every beer afficiando knows that stout and oysters is a terrific, classic pairing. And it's a stretch to accuse stout of being light and delicate. Sure, one is beer, the other is wine. But the point is that while rules and guidelines are helpful, they're not absolute. Each of us has our own peculiar palate.

Historically, Russians and Germans have favored wines that are far sweeter than those generally enjoyed in France or Spain. Italians appreciate wines with high acidity, while Californians and Australians steer away from them. Our sense of taste is an incredibly complex set of reactions incorporating everything from social customs to ingredients to temperature to memory to when we last brushed our teeth. In other words, it's both extremely personal and widely variable.

Do you love a good hot dog now and then? In Chicago, that would mean "pairing" your frank with onion, bright green sweet relish, hot peppers, a pickle spear, tomato slices, yellow mustard and celery salt. In Phoenix you'll get it bacon-wrapped with pinto beans, mayo, some queso fresco, jalapeños, and guacamole. New Englanders love their Coney Island dogs, covered in minced meat, mustard and steamed onions. Buy a dog on the streets of New York and it's topped with sauerkraut, maybe mustard and ketchup and minced onion to boot. Down South it's likely to be smothered in coleslaw. So who's right and who's wrong?

Exactly. No one. And everyone. It's a matter of taste, not tyranny.

To wit:

A beer drinker has but recently taken up the pleasures of wine. She (or he) joins a group, a table, a conference of business clients or associates, or of friends and acquaintances. "Shall we share a bottle?" she inquires. "Of course," comes the collective reply, followed by, "Have you a suggestion?"

Ha—it's like shooting fish in a barrel. And it's here that her (or your) hipness really begins to shine.

First tip: Relax—and enjoy. Wine is about pleasure and fun and good times as much as it's about anything. In any group, one or two people will immediately disqualify themselves from choosing a wine for everyone else to share. It's like an auto race and two of your competitors spin out on the first lap.

Second tip: Smile—and make it clear you're happy to choose the wine. Stepping up—i.e., assuming the "burden"—takes the pressure off the others and makes everyone feel good.

And if you're a rank beginner, disclose. (Remember, this is nothing more than a fleeting good time.) "To be honest, though, I should tell you the only wines I really know much about are Sauvignon Blancs from New Zealand and Merlots and Cabernet Sauvignons from Washington state."

"That's more than I know."

"That's probably more than most of us know!"

"So let's have one of those."

See. Girls (and guys) just wanna have fun. Don't sweat the small stuff. You might start by asking what kind or style of wine the others like. And no doubt you'll get a few in-depth answers like "red" or "white." But someone might mention a country or a type, Italian or something juicy but not too strong. Hint: when novice drinkers refer to a wine as strong, they usually mean a full-bodied, tannic red as much as they mean one with high alcohol.

If one or more of your mates answers "Australian Shiraz," you know at least one person is in the market for something fruity and rich; if another yells out "Châteauneuf-du-Pape" and you know nothing about Châteauneuf-du-Pape, just say "okay." In fact, until you've accumulated a pretty good body of wine knowledge, it's perfectly acceptable to fall back on a number of standard selections when choosing wine for a group.

If you're sharing a meal and everyone is having fish or chicken or something on the lighter side, an easy guideline is to select a white, possibly an unoaked Chardonnay (too much oak diminishes its ability to complement a wide range of foods). But another choice might be a New Zealand Sauvignon Blanc (though good Sauvignon Blanc is also produced in California, and a French Sancerre or Pouilly-Fumé is always a great expression of that variety) or a Pinot Gris from Oregon or Alsace.

Riesling can be an excellent choice as well, though you should know if the wine being considered is dry or has some degree of sweetness, and how your fellow drinkers feel about sweet wine. Those who like sweet wines tend to love them; those who don't, find them horrible. The best bets for dry Rieslings are Australia, Austria and Alsace—couldn't make that much easier to remember—and for those with some sweetness, look to Germany or even Washington.

Should everyone's food selection revolve around meat—steak, prime rib, lamb, burgers, ribs, etc.—you can safely choose almost any good red: a Burgundy or an Oregon Pinot Noir, Cabernet Sauvignon from Australia, California, Washington or Chile, Malbec (Argentinian, of course), Syrah or Grenache or various blends thereof from somewhere in either southern France or Australia. All delicious, all great with a variety of hearty foods.

Don't make it more complicated than it needs to be. *Calma,* baby.

Matching weight and texture is a pretty good start to food-and-wine pairing. Rich, heavy foods go well with rich, heavy wines. Conversely, light food and light wine seem to likewise enjoy each other's company.

Spicy food benefits from a bit of sweetness in a wine, be it a red Zinfandel with some residual sugar, a fruity Shiraz or an off-dry Gewurztraminer or Riesling.

The dominant flavor in many dishes comes from the sauce, so consider a citrusy wine with a lemony sauce. Or don't. Try anything that sounds interesting; find the matches *you* like.

If you enjoy tannins and chilies or full-bodied, high-alcohol wines with oysters on the half-shell, so what? It's your palate. Keep experimenting. You'll figure out what you do and don't like—without the rules.

And by the way, a little inside info: Champagne *does* go with just about everything!

And if your crew has chosen a mix of fish and fowl and meat and veggie dishes—those dirty rats—reach for the universal: Pinot Noir. Good Pinot has gorgeous red fruit flavors and great acidity, so it makes an almost-fail-safe food wine. Another great choice might be that previously mentioned juicy Grenache, perhaps from Australia or maybe Spain (the grape's homeland where, as you may recall, it's known as *Garnacha*). It's medium-bodied, red-fruit-for-ward, with typically high alcohol (good and bad at the same time), low tannins and an easy-going but distinctive personality.

The real key is to not panic. It's just grape juice. In the long run, who cares whether it was merely a good selection or a great one? It's wine, a gift, a wonderful anomaly of nature. Take a look at a bunch of grapes—who'da thunk it? Who would have imagined that this tight, compact, self-contained cluster of berries had the power to produce one of humankind's most important, and earliest, comforting, mind-altering restoratives? Think of the thanks due Mother Nature, in whatever guise she has most recently adopted.

■ ■ ■ ■

13

Wine Cocktails: Elegance Even the Snobs Miss Out On

I can count on one hand the number of wine cocktails that other grape nuts have offered me in umpteen years of serious wine imbibery. A shame, really. Other than the occasional brunch mimosa, a dastardly drink that mixes acid with acid and allows the offending restaurant to offload its cheapest bubbly, finding a big yumster wine cocktail is like hunting a needle in a fermentation tank. In other words, don't hold your breath.

The most famous, of course, are built around Champagne. And while it's perfectly acceptable to substitute a good Cava, cremant, or other sparkling wine, it's never okay to use lousy wine—for anything!

Harry's Bar in Venice, Italy, is the birthplace of the much-admired **Bellini**, a simple concoction of Prosecco (it's Italy, folks) and white peach juice (or pureed white peaches). Pour 1 part, or 2 oz., of peach juice into a Champagne flute and gently pour 2 parts, or 4 oz., of Prosecco on top. Best enjoyed overlooking the Grand Canal while listening to the gondoliers sing.

Prosecco is likewise the star and main ingredient of the **Amore Frizzante**. Other ingredients include 1 oz. of vodka, ½ oz. of orange liqueur, ½ oz. of peach nectar, and peach slices and raspberries to garnish. Pour the vodka, orange and peach liqueurs into a cocktail shaker filled with ice, shake vigorously for 10 seconds or so, and strain into a chilled Champagne flute. Top with Prosecco and garnish with fruit. The result is surprisingly complex.

Another wine cocktail of long standing is the **Kir Royale**, a classy aperitif composed of 1 part Crème de Cassis (black-currant liqueur) in a Champagne flute or white wine glass and 6 to 8 parts dry Champagne poured over it. Think elegance, Euro-style.

For a more down-home but unquestionably tasty "Dubliner" version of the above, opt for a **Black Velvet**. Fill a champagne flute halfway with chilled Guinness (or any good stout) and pour an equal amount of Champagne, slowly and carefully, perhaps over the dome of an inverted spoon so the two don't mix, to fill. Sounds a bit odd; it's really scrumptious.

Hint: if you honestly have a thing for **Mimosas**, try substituting strawberry juice for orange juice. It works so much better. But keep in mind that not all wine cocktails need contain bubbles. Here are a few using white or red still wine as a base.

A great refresher is the **Zealander**. Start with 3 oz. of good-quality Sauvignon Blanc in a cocktail shaker. Add to this ½ oz. of grapefruit juice, ½ oz. of lemon juice, a teaspoon or so of simple syrup, and a couple dashes of Angostura® Bitters. Add ice, shake, and strain into a highball glass filled with cubes. Add club soda to top.

Or if you're in a Spanish mood, mix up a **White Sangria**. Into a pitcher goes 4 oz. of dry white wine, 2 oz. of lemon-lime soda, ¼ oz. Triple Sec, and one teaspoon of sugar (adjust to taste). Stir, being sure to dissolve the sugar, pour over ice—almost any stemmed beer glass is ideal—and garnish with slices of orange and lemon.

And who can overlook the **One-Balled Dictator**, a gift of humor and good drinking from some WWII Army Air Corps boys—be careful how you ask someone if they'd like one. Mix 5 parts chilled Liebfraumilch (a not terribly sweet German wine) with 1 part chilled Champagne, shake with extreme gusto and pour into a rocks glass over a single red-hot cinnamon ball. Both a visual and gustatory experience.

For your best girlfriends or that one special lady, put together a **Glamour Girl**. Pour 3 oz. of dry pale rosé wine, 1 oz. of peach schnapps and a splash of cranberry juice into a cocktail shaker filled with ice. Shake and pour into a chilled martini glass. Garnish with a cherry. Gorgeous color and a darned good drink.

For you red-wine cocktailers (using good but not Latour-good wine), a reasonable starting point is the **French Monkey**. Into a highball glass half-filled with ice, pour 2 parts red wine and 1 part Orangina® orange soda, cold. This one is great for chillin' on the front porch.

The **Bishop Cocktail** starts with a lemon slice and ¾ oz. of simple syrup in your cocktail shaker. Muddle—crush, gently mangle, prod with authority—the lemon wheel to extract not only the juice but also the essential oils in the peel, add 1 part, or 2 oz., of white rum, half fill with ice, shake vigorously, and strain into a stemmed goblet. Then pour 2 parts, or 4 oz., of full-bodied red wine on top and garnish with half a lemon slice. Quick—fix me another!

Recently discovered is the **Gran Piemonte**. Into your shaker add 2 oz. of good Barbera, 1 oz. of any Highland Scotch whisky (for just the right waft of peaty smoke), 1 oz. brewed black tea that's been chilled, ½ oz. of simple syrup, and ½ oz. of lemon juice. Fill with ice, shake and strain into a rocks glass over a couple of cubes. Garnish with a dash of freshly grated nutmeg.

The **Berry Happy To See You** begins with ½ cup of frozen raspberries, ½ cup of frozen blackberries, 5 oz. of Zinfandel,

1½ oz. of silver tequila, 1 oz. of simple syrup, and 1 teaspoon of fresh lime juice. Put all the makings into a blender and mix until the berries are liquefied. Pour into a tall glass half-filled with ice, through a strainer to remove the berry seeds. Garnish with orange slice and fresh berries. This one is berry, berry good.

Many thanks to the originators of these drinks, most of whom are lost to either posterity or the muddle of the millions of variations on their tasty handiwork. We may not know your names, but we drink to your efforts nonetheless. Thank you, one and all.

By the way, don't overlook beer cocktails, which have moved way beyond the classic Black and Tan (stout and ale) or Snakebites (cider and lager), thanks in part to the large number of craft brews now available on tap. Bartenders no longer need open a pricey bottle for a few ounces; with taps they can mix beer drinks just like any other cocktails—and they are! Ask at your local watering hole and see what the resident mixologist is into these days. You might be pleasantly surprised.

■ ■ ■ ■

14

The Right Stuff—Goodies, Gadgets & Accessories: What You Do Need & What You Definitely Don't

Sooner or later you'll notice the sheer quantity of must-have gadgets associated with wine drinking. It's a bit like golf: a thousand goofy gizmos all claiming to improve your game. For the duffer that means weeding through umpteen varieties of golf bags, a thousand styles of putters, snap-on scorekeepers to attach to bag or cart, better fitting gloves, eco-friendly golf shoes, training aids that wrap you in slings and cables like you've had both arms broken, club face stickers to mark the ball's point of impact, putting cups and carpets, golf ball retrievers, personalized shaft labels, range finders, head covers, shoe and club cleaning kits, practice nets, drink dispensers, beverage holders, magnetic bracelets, golf ball cleaners, even "performance" tees (how—are they battery-operated?) Makes you wonder how the greats of old ever managed a decent round of golf devoid of the wonders of modern living.

And yet they did, all of them—Arnold Palmer, Bobby Jones, Sam Snead, Babe Zaharia—before most of the items listed above had even been invented. The vast majority of all this indispensible "stuff" spilling from catalogs and pro shops alike does more for the sellers' bottom line than for the golfer's handicap. And so it is with wine accessories.

Instead of the head covers and swing trainers, wine aficionados are confronted with dozens of styles of decanters, personalized "chateau" plaques, grape-themed calendars, lamps, floor mats, coasters and napkins, bottle stoppers, pourers, preservers, funnels and screens, bags and totes, cork boards, label savers and bottle tags, not to mention chillers and racks and wax whackers and a thousand types of corkscrews to go with a thousand types of wine glasses. Again, how did those long-ago Rothschilds and Medicis manage to enjoy the great vintages of the past minus cutesy good-luck charms around the stems of their glasses?

Hard to say. Though it seems they did.

A few items are essential, and a few are just cool. Everything else seems little more than a waste of good money better spent on wine. Or maybe a few bottles of that Belgian monster you've been wanting to try.

Here are the essentials:

Corkscrews: So many corkscrews of so many types have been developed through the ages that people actually collect them, some owning hundreds of these must-have devices in collections worth thousands of dollars. Once you start drinking wine on a regular basis, however, these clever little gadgets will find their way into your life, most of them of inferior quality and best thrown away, especially when one or two of the "right" kind will more than suffice.

What constitutes the right kind depends. On you. A style called the straight-pull, usually a simple T-handle device, takes a good deal of strength if a cork decides to be at all stubborn.

A lever and gear style, on the other hand, the so-called Rabbit® being the best-known, will easily extract almost any cork, though they cost on the order of $40 or $50 compared to $3 or $4 for most straight-pull types. Yet, they are such slick pieces of engineering that you'll want one. There are even large table-mounted corkscrews with gears and chrome-plated handles designed for wine bars or serious wine cellars.

Straight-pull   *Rabbit*   *Waiters' friend*

Cork popper   *Wing lever*   *Electric corkscrew*

A favored opener, or wine "key," as they're called in the restaurant business, is the "waiters' friend" corkscrew, with a folding screw, aka "the worm," and a small attached knife blade for cutting the foil or plastic capsule away from the cork. These are versatile, fairly inexpensive, and quite efficient. Another common though less effective model has two winged levers that splay out as you twist the worm into the cork. Once the screw is set, pulling down on the levers will, if all goes well, extract the cork. Kinda cool in action, rather awkward to use. A smoother related version, sans wings, operates by continuing to twist the worm until the cork is slowly pulled up and out of the bottle.

A bit of fun can be had with the needle-and-gas cork popper. A long, hollow needle is inserted through the cork and a button pushed on this compact device's gas cartridge and—presto!—a propellant gas instantly fills the bottle and out pops the cork. Admittedly, the novelty wears off after opening half a dozen bottles and there's the occasional hassle of picking up replacement cartridges (though each opens about seventy bottles), but it's a definite crowd-pleaser and quick and easy to use.

One modern development, the perfect solution for anyone with weak or arthritic hands, is the electric push-button corkscrew. Just set this cylinder down over the bottle top, push the button, and the cork is quickly and easily powered out. If you suffer from carpal tunnel syndrome or have any kind of hand problem, these units are ideal.

Some corkscrews include a foil cutter—as the capsule around the neck of the bottle usually has to be cut away under the bottle's lip to allow access to the cork itself—and some do not. If yours doesn't, a small foil cutter is a cheap, effective necessity to add to your accessories collection.

A final note on corkscrews: if you travel often, any corkscrew with a built-in knife blade, even one only half an inch long, will be confiscated by airport security personnel should it be in your carry-on bag. Either snap the blade off your "traveling model" prior to entering the security line or opt for the compact, inexpensive T- handle to take along in your on-board luggage.

Wine racks: The next thing to consider might be a rack for storing your new purchases, instead of just standing the bottles on a kitchen counter or leaving them in a box in the corner of your dining room. Be it a six-, twelve-, or twenty-bottle rack, this approach puts the wine on its side, where it belongs (which, as mentioned, keeps the corks wet so they don't dry out and begin to shrink, compromising the seal and letting oxygen into the wine). But whatever you do, don't put your nifty little rack on top of the refrigerator or near the stove or next to a radiator. Remember, the one thing wine hates is excess heat; in fact, there's no quicker way to ruin a good bottle of juice than to let it get too warm. Cook the food, not the wine. That said, even a cheap and simple wine rack that holds only a few bottles is worth the investment.

Once you get more involved in wine, you might start looking at wine coolers or refrigerators. Some hold no more than half a dozen bottles and cost as little as $40 or $50. Others can be über appliances standing six feet tall and holding a few hundred bottles. Storage temperature doesn't mean as much if you drink everything within three or four days of buying it, but if you're going to start collecting, it makes sense to take care of your purchases. The ideal temperature to set the cooler at is 55° F, though a degree or two either way won't make any difference. Read the reviews and choose a brand that other wine lovers seem to like. A quiet motor and a good thermostat are the keys.

Glasses: Now that you have a place to keep your wine and a way to open the bottles (i.e., your chosen corkscrew, and that needle-and-gas cork popper kept around for a little extra pizzazz—high coolness factor—when you might need it), it's time to look at glasses. After all, beer drinker or not, there are precious few situations where sucking the Vino Nobile di Montepulciano directly from the bottle is the desired approach.

While jelly glasses are a step up and various beer mugs, pilsners and tulips have been used in a pinch, good wine is worthy of good glassware. Just as a beer tulip is designed to help support the head of a good pour, well-made wine glasses help concentrate the aromas of the wine. And virtually all good wine has much to offer in the aroma department.

The conventional wisdom is that it's best to avoid glasses with straight or open contours. Examples include the coupette, the shallow martini-type Champagne glass said to be inspired by the breasts of Marie Antoinette, or other aesthetically pleasing (or is it pleading?) etched or painted or oddly shaped glassware, which may be beautiful to behold but falls short when it comes time to show off the best of a particular wine.

A good glass is well-balanced, nicely shaped, flared at mid-hip to provide surface area within the glass for the wine to "stretch out," and then tapers to a somewhat smaller opening, concentrating the wine's aromas. If you favor red wine, a larger bowl is probably the better choice, and if you drink mostly white or rosé, a tighter bowl will focus the less phenolic wine for increased enjoyment. If you can, pick up a glass before you buy a set, whether it's four, six, or more; it should feel natural to you, neither top- nor bottom-heavy, easy to handle, thin-rimmed. The best glasses practically beg you to give them a pour of something terrific just by their weight and feel in your hand. And don't buy one or two. Take a splurge and get half a dozen. Or a dozen. You're going to break a few, as we all do. With enough glasses on hand, you'll be more likely to invite friends over to try your latest vinous discovery. After all, wine drinking at its best is a communal affair.

Stoppers and preservation systems: There will be times—rare, perhaps, but possible nonetheless—when a bottle will be opened and remain unfinished. What to do? Assuming it's good wine, in most cases just pushing the cork back in and leaving the bottle on a table or counter is not the best idea. The wine is now exposed to oxygen and will begin a rather rapid deterioration; just how rapid depends on the particular wine. Some will remain in fairly good shape for a day, maybe two. But others will be spoiled by the next morning, so why chance ruining wine that you enjoyed and paid for?

The most commonly used preserver is a Vacu-Vin, which consists of a rubber stopper and a small hand pump. Push the stopper into the bottle, set the pump on top and give it a few good pumps. The reusable stopper is designed so that the pump sucks out most of the air and leaves a sealed bottle. This will extend the life of the wine for an additional day or two.

Even better is a small can of nitrogen or argon (available at wine shops as Vineyard Fresh, Wine Preserver or Private Preserve) and some good lever-top bottle stoppers. Squirt a few shots of inert gas into the bottle and snap a stopper in place. Many wine lovers find this system will add a couple more days to a wine's drinkable life than the Vacu-Vin. And either approach requires an outlay of only about ten dollars U.S.

Hint, hint: eke out an extra day with either of these systems by storing the bottle upright in a refrigerator and then letting it warm to room temperature before pouring the remaining wine. It's such a waste to pour leftover juice down the drain. It's meant to go down the hatch, so preserving an open bottle is not just smart but cool and economical.

Decanters: Speaking of cool, decanters may look it, but are they really necessary? Well, there are two situations where pouring wine into a decanter will clearly improve the drinking to follow. The first is when serving a young, full-bodied, highly tannic wine, say a newly released Cabernet Sauvignon-dominant Bordeaux or a massive Brunello di Montalcino. As delicious as these wines are, the sometimes-monstrous tannins can be over-powering, to the point where it's hard to discern the fruit or the elegance of what will be a wonderful wine once it ages and all its elements come into balance.

When decanting for this purpose there's no need to pour slowly and carefully. Just upend the bottle and splash the wine into its new container. The whole idea is to agitate the wine and increase its surface area so as to get more oxygen into it. Done a couple of hours before serving, this will soften the harshness of the tannins and increase the wine's overall complexity. And there's something sexy about pouring your guests' wine from a cool-looking decanter you've set on the table.

As you may have guessed, the other circumstance that benefits from the use of a decanter is when opening older bottles, where the wine has "thrown" a deposit of sediment. This can be seen as a dark coating on the inside of the bottle along the side it's been resting on. While this sediment is harmless, a mouthful of it is decidedly unpleasant and hardly the way to enjoy a mature wine at its peak of drinkability. It's that sediment you want to get rid of.

As opposed to decanting young reds where the object is aeration, when handling older bottles before decanting you should attempt to keep the bottle "quiet" so as not to disturb the sediment. In front of a strong light so you can see through the bottle, commence pouring the wine slowly, steadily and gently into the decanter. As you near the bottom of the bottle, keep an eye peeled for sediment starting to run into the stream of wine—and stop once you see it. That's it. You've barred all that nasty sediment from getting into the decanter or the glasses to be poured from it. There may be half an inch of wine left in the bottle or an inch and a half. In any case, mission accomplished. Just discard what remains and enjoy your decanted wine.

As with corkscrews, there are many styles of decanters. They range from short and squat to tall and swan-necked. As long as they pour well and provide good surface area for the wine, no one design is better than any other. Find one you like that you can handle easily; beyond that it's just a matter of taste.

▪ *TECHNICAL DRIVEL* ▪

Oxygen's initial effect on wine is to round out those "hard edges," to accelerate its aging, if you will. Of course, once something begins to age, it's on the path that eventually leads to spoilage. Hence the need to delay unchecked oxygenation by means of gas or a Vacu-Vin for wine that's being saved for another day. Think of it as a "ripening" process: green fruit isn't very tasty, but let it mature and it becomes sweet and succulent; yet let it mature for too long and it begins to rot.

In the case of red wine, part of the aging process is the joining together of molecules of tannin and color compounds into long chains too heavy to remain suspended in liquid. These overgrown polymers "precipitate" or fall out of suspension and settle to the bottom or sides of a bottle as sediment. It's for this reason that older red wines have less tannin and lighter color than young red wines.

And all that other stuff: There's not much else you really need once you can buy your wine, store it, open it and drink it. As long as you're enjoying it. Try different wines from different regions. There's a wonderful variety and diversity in the world of wines. And most are made to be enjoyed for multiple glasses, many as an accompaniment to food. You may find yourself picking up wine magazines or checking out wine videos online. All good. Just never cut your own preferences short in favor of what some critic "declares." At the same time, don't fall for the adage that the "best" wine is the wine you like. That's foolishness, and self-pandering.

What you like is what you like, and you need make no apologies for it. But that doesn't mean it's the best wine. Taste in wine evolves as one gathers more information, more experience.

What you like when first being exposed to good wine will in all probability be quite different a year or two later. For a new driver, a comfortable, easy-to-handle sports sedan could well be the favored vehicle, but it's unlikely that anyone would call that a "better" car than a Rolls Royce or Lamborghini. For many people, though, the sports sedan would be a better expenditure, a wiser use of limited funds. So buy what you like, what you're comfortable with, but stay open and on the lookout for new varieties, new vintages and new wine regions.

As to all the other accessories, accoutrements, gizmos, gadgets and tchotchkes, knock yourself out. If you like something, pick it up. But realize that a metal tab dunked in new wine doesn't make it the equivalent of an oak-aged cuvee, that fancy etched or hand-painted glasses may look interesting but seldom do much for the wine, that wine writers have opinions—like all of us—but not a mandate from above to anoint the "best." It's grape juice with a kick, kids! Don't get carried away. Pour a glass and enjoy.

■ ■ ■ ■

15

Parting (& Partying) Thoughts

Now that you're supremely cool, wise and well-tutored in the world of fermented grape juice …

Wow, that sounds pretty obnoxious. Let's start over.

My hope is that *A Beer Drinker's Guide To Knowing And Enjoying Fine Wine* has been a worthwhile read. Wine, like beer, is a fabulous and complex beverage, with history, ceremony, art, science and deliciousness all contributing to its appeal. For wine and beer drinkers alike, this is a golden age. Quality gets better and better, and the choices—thanks to so many micro- and craft breweries and start-up wineries—are exploding. In the U.S., it's hard *not* to find great beer or terrific wine wherever you are. And the same can be said for much of the rest of the world.

It's important to encourage these entrepreneurs of taste to keep up the good work, to continue pushing the envelope. In that regard, the aficionados of both beer and wine can serve their own long-term interests by trying new brands, new labels, new producers. When store shelves hold hundreds of craft-brewed and vinified offerings, take a chance and pick up something new, something you haven't tried before. If you like it, buy it again, and if you don't, don't. Let the market—i.e., us, the consumers—speak. The best of these drink-makers, the most able and daring, will succeed, and the mere hangers-on with no real talent or passion, at least none that shines through in the bottle, won't.

Just as you're a fan of good beer, of its amber hue and spritzy, grain-rich aromas, of its flavors, be they bitter and hoppy, deep and roasted, or sweetly malty, so too will you come to crave a perfect glass of wine. It may be to accompany dinner or for relaxing by the pool, for dazzling and delighting your special someone, or for celebrating a job well done.

Remember that wine is best enjoyed with others. Pick up half a dozen different wines, lay out some cheese and nibbles, and invite your fifteen or twenty closest friends over—or anyone else who happens to be in the neighborhood. Pour, toast, celebrate, enjoy. Share what you've learned and spread your new enthusiasm around. The idea is to generate your own group of wine geeks (who might be hard-core beer swillers on other occasions) to test and try and perhaps even make it a regular thing.

The terrific thing about wine is that it keeps getting better. And that holds true on every level. The last sips of a good bottle are always better than the first. The new wines you try as you become more practiced and experienced are always better than the ones you started with. The Chardonnay or Syrah you love today is most likely a better wine than the Chardonnays and Syrahs you were drawn to at first.

There's a saying much admired by wine lovers (either considered a traditional Italian aphorism or attributed to everyone from Louis Pasteur to Omar Khayyam): "A day without wine is like a day without sunshine." For the initiated, nothing could be more true. But initiation isn't something you purchase or earn, nor is it dependent on how much you know or how extensively you've studied. It doesn't mean that you forgo other food or drink or that you've learned a secret handshake or changed your wardrobe or hairstyle.

One day a remarkable phenomenon will occur: a wine will speak to you. A vinepiphany, you might call it. A profound coming together of taste and aroma, of intellect and emotion, of instinct and curiosity. It will, in a flash, all make sense. You will know what great winemakers strive for. You will understand how, in an ancient world with few other drinks than milk, water, and if you were lucky, flat, unhopped beer, wine was regarded as a gift of the gods, especially as its creation required little human involvement and its consumption engendered feelings of euphoria. Why civilizations from Mesopotamia to ancient Greece held this simple, fermented fruit juice in such high esteem.

For whatever reason, that particular wine will strike all your chords simultaneously. It's a holistic experience. You'll wish your glass never to be empty. You'll be struck dumb by the glory of a perfect moment.

You will then be initiated.

Ever after, your wine experiences will refer back to that instance. Ask any dyed-in-the-wool devotee when a wine first rocked his or her world and they'll be able to tell you. Often the wine, the vintage, the place and the circumstance.

Whether you began this vinous journey to satisfy a spouse, a boss, or your own curiosity, you're well on your way. Reread and review. Taste and travel. And never be intimidated. If you've gathered anything from this book, I hope it's that wine is a joy, one of the benefits of a good life and not some snobby pursuit intended to keep others out. Because wherever and whatever I'm drinking, I'd rather share a glass with someone like you than drink alone. *Salud!*

■ ■ ■ ■

Index

Enjoy learning about wine?

Order additional copies directly from
Crosstown Publishing at

<u>www.crosstownpublishinginc.com</u>

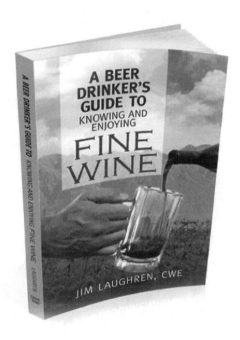

Ask about discount pricing for bulk purchases.

- Gift shops
- Wine schools
- Tasting groups
- Culinary schools
- Winery tasting rooms

- Wine & liquor stores
- Breweries & brew pubs
- Corporate promotions
- Industry training
- Travel agencies